THERE
IS
A
WAY
OUT!

ABOUT THE AUTHOR

"How would you feel if the troubles and tensions of life were suddenly lifted from your shoulders? With persistent pursuit of truthful principles, that delightful feeling can be yours." That is a summary of the exciting message Vernon Howard has given over the years in his books and lectures. More than six million readers have experienced the power of Mr. Howard's books and tapes, including translations into French, German, Spanish, Italian, Portuguese and Japanese. Vernon Howard's clear insight into human problems, and his practical solutions, attract thousands of new readers every year.

Groups of men and women who study Vernon Howard's teachings are located throughout the United States and Canada. The classes study Mr. Howard's books and listen to his taped lectures. Those who wish information on these meetings can write to New Life (address below).

INVITATION

Please send us the names and
addresses of friends who may be
interested in these helpful teachings.
We will send them our free literature.
Write to:
NEW LIFE
BOX 684
BOULDER CITY, NEVADA 89005

THERE
IS
A
WAY
OUT!

vernon howard

DeVORSS & CO., *Publishers*
Box 550
Marina del Rey, California 90291

Vernon Howard lives and
teaches in Boulder City, Nevada.
For information on classes, books,
tapes and video cassettes, write:
NEW LIFE
BOX 684
BOULDER CITY, NEVADA 89005

CONTENTS

HOW TO USE THIS BOOK
FOR RICHER LIVING

Is there a way out of confusion and a way into life-prosperity? Of course there is. You are about to discover the ways with a fascinating journey which begins right now.

In these pages you will hear questions and comments from all kinds of people—from the sincere and the anxious, from those who yearn for the way out and from those who have found it. You will then hear answers—answers which you will sense as being wonderfully friendly and helpful.

This book is a new and dynamic contribution to the self-help field. The short and inspiring items come right to the point—the point being self-newness for all who want it.

Use these practical plans: 1. Consult the Sixty Guides on page 9 to locate and solve specific problems. 2. Remember that each item contains more value than appears at first, so look for pleasant surprises of hidden gold during future months of reading. 3. Use these truths in daily affairs, letting them enlighten and change your inner nature. 4. Join or form a study group whose members have an enthusiasm for exploring the way out. 5. Adventure forward with confidence and good cheer, for regardless of anyone's present condition, there is a way out.

Vernon Howard
Boulder City, Nevada

SIXTY INSPIRING GUIDES

Select a subject listed below and turn to the page and title indicated. Read and reflect upon the information supplied. Use these guides for both individual exploration and for group discussions.

1. To discover a valuable secret known by those who have found the way out: see page 59 WHAT MUST BE DONE.

2. For building an inner confidence which nothing can shake: see page 94 REAL CONFIDENCE.

3. Why you should remain encouraged over the inner adventure: see page 29 THE NEXT STEP.

4. If you wish to create a bright and favorable tomorrow: see page 170 FUTURE.

5. For staying out of trouble in the first place: see page 14 COSMIC SCIENCE.

6. How to find a mental state of peace and contentment: see page 123 REST YOUR MIND.

7. If you ever feel doubtful about yourself and your life: see page 57 SELF-DOUBT.

8. For a fact that has a deeper meaning than appears on the surface: see page 151 EVERYTHING CAN BE DONE.

9. To find a source of true and inspiring guidance: see page 124 ACCURATE SOURCE.

10. If you wish to read about the fascinating process of self-recovery: see page 141 NATURAL HEALING.

11. For important information about a life of pleasant independence: see page 72 THE WILD HORSE.

12. How to use these principles profitably when earning your living: see page 53 CONSCIOUS BUSINESSMAN.

13. When you want a principle that will guide you all the way out: see page 134 REASONS FOR UNHAPPINESS.

14. How to attain successes you may now believe impossible: see page 100 FLIGHT.

31. To learn about a great opportunity to make everything new: see page 32 MAGIC MOMENT!

32. How foolish and misguiding beliefs are acquired: see page 143 THE WITNESS.

33. For victory over all kinds of anxiety: see page 111 HOW TO BE UNAFRAID.

34. How to think about your problems constructively and without tension: see page 82 SELF-RECOVERY.

35. If you want a rule for living which keeps you in the right: see page 41 NATURAL AGREEMENT.

36. How one man replaced painful self-conflict with peaceful self-unity: see page 132 MASKS.

37. To read a story with a tremendous lesson for all who seek self-release: see page 106 ENTER THE ROOM.

38. How to proceed calmly and correctly through every day: see page 87 HANDLING DAILY EVENTS.

39. To place your feelings on the side of self-victory: see page 163 THE SENSIBLE MAN.

40. For an experiment that awakens independent thinking: see page 117 HOW TO THINK FOR YOURSELF.

41. How to prevent yourself from being victimized by deceitful people: see page 63 VICTIMS.

42. Why you should never feel that life has denied you anything: see page 138 MISSING OUT.

43. For a practical program which makes everything easier to understand: see page 164 EXERCISE IN CLARITY.

44. When you do not know how to handle depression: see page 79 THE PROBLEM OF GLOOM.

45. To read an encouraging fact about self-upliftment: see page 97 HOW SELF-INSIGHT ADVANCES.

46. Why a person attracts into his life the kind of people who are there: see page 67 LIKE ATTRACTS LIKE.

47. If your life seems forced and unnatural: see page 144 THE RIGHT RING.

48. To learn about the success of those who have found the way out: see page 68 HIDDEN WATER.

49. When you need to remember the power of receptivity: see page 158 SAFE HARBOR.

50. To discover the aim of a man who really knows the truth: see page 155 COME OUT OF HIDING.

51. How to have a new and different kind of fun that lasts: see page 19 FUN.

52. To rise above your present life to see a new world: see page 128 REAL HAPPINESS.

53. Why gullibility must be studied and brought to an end: see page 99 FOX AND SHEEP.

54. If you wish to act with ease in everyday situations: see page 140 TWO TIGERS.

55. For attaining a self-command that controls threatening circumstances: see page 81 SELF-COMMAND.

56. When you want to remain calm and competent in business matters: see page 34 EARNING A LIVING.

57. For information about a progressively enjoyable experience: see page 145 PLEASANTLY ASTOUNDING.

58. To remind yourself of what these teachings are all about: see page 13 THE STAR.

59. For vital facts about locating an authentic source of help: see page 40 HOW TO FIND A TRUE TEACHER.

60. To read and explore these ideas with maximum efficiency: see page 56 STUDY METHOD.

Chapter 1

POWERFUL FACTS ABOUT THE WAY OUT

THE STAR

"What are these teachings all about?"

"Imagine yourself standing in your home at night while gazing out the window through slightly parted curtains. You see a brilliant star. If you lean to either left or right of your position you cut off sight of the star. We are teaching ourselves to stand in just the right cosmic position to see something higher than ourselves. Can you think of a more fascinating adventure?"

SELF-KNOWLEDGE

"I don't know the way out."

"*You* are the way out."

"I don't know what that means."

"Know yourself and you will know."

WHOLENESS

"I wish to be whole, but am not sure what this means."

"Wholeness is the harmonious working of all the natural parts of a man. This includes thoughts, feelings, physical movements, sexual urges, action, speech, and so on. An obsession is the domination of one wild part over the other parts, as when sex dominates the mind or when impulsive emotions dictate violent action. Knowledge of all this is the beginning of self-wholeness and thus self-command."

COSMIC SCIENCE

"Just what is this teaching?"

"It can be accurately called Cosmic Science."

"In a practical way, what does it do?"

"It keeps you from falling into trouble in the first place."

"That alone makes it worthwhile."

STAGE PERFORMANCE

"What is human life like?"

"Like a gigantic stage performance, which a story will illustrate. A group of children often played a game of dramatics in which each portrayed a stage character. One played the role of an important person, another of a profound thinker, and so on. Then they grew up. Incredibly, they continued to play their roles, which they now took as realities. They went around acting as if they were important or profound. They felt depressed and angry when other people did not accept their roles as real. They sensed that something was wrong, but did not know what it was."

SELF HONESTY

"We all agree on the necessity of persistent self-honesty. Where might a beginner help himself?"

"He can ask whether he really enjoys his life, or whether he painfully endures it because he knows not what else to do."

PRELIMINARY STAGE

"When first trying to find the way out I attended all kinds of meetings—religious, philosophical, and some quite weird. I finally realized something you have told us repeatedly in this class. You said we find what we unconsciously wish to find. You know what I foolishly wished to find? Excitement and entertainment. Now I know better."

"That was a necessary preliminary stage."

ATTENTION

"I have failed to become a financial success."

"Place your attention elsewhere."

"I fear that someone I love may leave me."

"Place your attention elsewhere."

"To what should I attend?"

"To ways for rising above self-torture. Listen to me. I will show you how right attention can make you a king."

SUNSHINE

"I hope my spirit is not too dark to learn."

"How you underestimate yourself! You always forget that while you are your own darkness you are also your own sunshine for ending the darkness."

THE FIGHTING FOX

"I now see how I used to fight against my own liberation."

"Yes, the facts we fight the most are the very ones we need the most. This is one of the most incredible features of miserable man. He fights and fears the very medicine which could cure him."

"Why does he do this?"

"It connects with his foolish defense of false positions. A fox fights when you get close to the stolen goods he is hiding in his den."

THE STRANGE OBJECT

"It is true that we scorn that which we do not understand."

"A wind carried a man's hat deep into the woods where man had never visited. Gathering around the hat, the wild creatures tried to discover its use. A dove thought it was a nest, while a bear declared it to be a strange and huge berry. Every animal but one connected the hat with his own personal needs and experiences. The exception was a wise owl who immediately identified the strange object as a hat. The owl explained that he had been in another part of the woods where creatures called men wore hats all the time. Never having heard of a man before, the creatures derided the owl and continued to be puzzled over the hat.''

WHAT IS NEEDED

''I know I need something but can never find it.''
''How strange that you do not see what is so close.''
''See what?''
''That what you need is your own nature, liberated from illusions and pretenses.''
''It is dawning on me that what I take as true and what is actually true are as far apart as earth and sun.''

FIRST LESSON

''I wish to enter your school of cosmic wisdom.''
''Come back in three weeks.''
''Here I am, three weeks later.''
''Come back in six weeks.''
''Here I am, six weeks later.''
''You may now receive your second lesson.''
''But what was my first?''
''The ability to take rejection.''

YOUR LIFE

''I am caught between loyalty to my traditional beliefs and my urge to break out.''
''Do not feel guilty about leaving the old. You owe nothing to illusions. Do not permit other slaves to keep you in chains. Your life belongs to you and you alone.''
''But what should I accept and what should be rejected?''
''You are never required to accept anything you have not seen or experienced for yourself.''

NEW READING HABITS

"Many interesting changes have occurred in my reading habits since attending these classes. Not only do I read completely different kinds of books, but I read in a new way."

"Yes, that always happens. Reading most books is like strolling idly down a country lane. No special thinking or feeling is required; you just follow wherever led. But esoteric reading is unique. It is like stepping off the country lane to explore unfamiliar ground. You must pause and look and examine. The customary country lane will lead you, but only unfamiliar ground can change you."

PERMISSION

"Can you really help me?"

"Will you really permit me?"

ASLEEP AND AWAKE

"I do not fully understand what it means to be spiritually asleep or awake."

"To be asleep means to be the slave of anger and envy, to demand that events turn out according to personal desire, to deceive oneself and others, to suffer from guilt and shame, to take secret delight in hurting others, to live in fear. To be awake means to possess self-understanding, to have only one person within yourself, to see through the folly of worldly ambitions, to live from your real nature, to be free of all negative feelings, to be genuinely compassionate."

CONDITIONING

"You seem to say we must leave our own intelligence behind when coming to these classes."

"Do not confuse intelligence with conditioning."

"Why can't we bring our acquired ideas?"

"Can fire and water mix?"

LEAF OF TRUTH

"What should we do with an offered truth?"

"Four men walked through the Forest of Truth together. A leaf bearing a sublime message fluttered down at their feet. The scholar said he would write a long book describing the shape and color of the leaf. The man who considered himself religious claimed that this was heaven's sign for him to go forth and save others. The angry man shouted his intention to fight the truth. But the fourth man merely read the message, nodded, and silently walked on. Nothing in him wanted to use the truth for personal profit."

THE DIFFERENCE

"What is the difference between these teachings and ordinary systems?"

"Ordinary systems condemn the driver as being evil because he bumped his car into a pole. These teachings say he bumped into the pole because he is spiritually asleep, psychologically unaware."

"But this does not mean that an individual is excused for his violent behavior."

"No. Any excuse for violence only promotes more violence. No excuses are accepted."

THE SHOP

"Society has thousands of plans for helping the helpless, but not much changes."

"Picture a shopkeeper standing in front of his shop and shouting to passersby about his delicious fruits and vegetables. But the shop is empty. That is society. Only the individual who has found himself has anything to give."

FIXED BEHAVIOR

"I have a certain fear that I might lose my own individuality by accepting these higher truths."

"Do you have individuality or do you merely have a fixed pattern of behavior which keeps you in conflict?"

"I see what you mean. Sheep in a flock may have different characteristics, but they are still sheep."

"If you could only see it, what you will lose is what a certain part of you yearns to lose."

"I will try to see it."

INSPIRATION

"I wish to be inspired."

"Then realize that inspiration is not the same as stimulation. Stimulation is temporary excitement, usually caused by exterior events. It always swings over to depression."

"And what is true inspiration?"

"A glimpse of truth hidden within you. It comes at first in a brief revelation, just as a flash of lightning illuminates the scene for a split second."

NEW VIEW!

"I don't know how to find the higher life."

"To win the higher give up the lower. The home of a man stood near a beautiful lake. Also on his property was an old and unused cabin which blocked the view of the lake from the home. The man took great pride in boasting to visitors about several famous men who had possibly spent a night in the cabin. At the same time he was saddened by his inability to see the rippling waters. He finally sacrificed his boasting by tearing down the cabin, which gave him a new view."

FUN

"I want my life to be fun."

"So?"

"Don't these studies tend to take away fun?"

"Is your present life fun?"

"No."

"Has it ever been fun?"

"No."

"These studies are the only real fun on earth."

THE JOLT

"For many years I lived in smug self-satisfaction. No one could tell me anything. Then came the jolt I feared would come. My world fell apart."

"What in particular did this jolt reveal?"

"The number of things I was hiding from myself."

"Yes, that is what must happen. You were jolted out of sleep, and now you are awakening."

"And about time."

LEAP OUT OF DARKNESS

"You have told other members of this class about individual fears which block progress. May I know which fear keeps me back?"

"The fear of appearing foolish. This includes both a fear of appearing foolish to yourself and to other people. You must therefore permit entrance of true ideas which may indeed make you look foolish. This is the only cure for both the fear and the feeling of foolishness. At first it appears like a terrible thing to do to yourself, but it is really a heroic leap out of darkness."

THRILLED PEOPLE

"Please discuss right and wrong attitudes toward a man who really knows what he is talking about."

"A famous teacher once gave a lecture to some people who had neither seen nor heard him before. Many in the audience were thrilled at seeing such a renowned person. A few others were thrilled by what he talked about. It was these few people who went away with something unpossessed before."

SEVEN KEYS

"I have seven keys in my hand, but do not know which one opens the door."

"Try them."

"But what if none of them work?"

"That is the whole story of apprehensive man. He fears that nothing exists beyond his petty ways. Courageously experiment until identifying the six wrong keys. The remaining key will work but you cannot know this until eliminating the wrong keys."

A SIMPLE FACT

"Why do some events make me feel happy, while others bring sadness?"

"Because some events seem to confirm false ideas you have about life, while others seem to deny them."

"Is it really as simple as that?"

"As simple as that. However, you must prove this for yourself through daily experience. For instance, notice your disturbance when other people do not agree with your claims of being a successful person. This leads to a state which is above all events."

IMITATION

"What prevents simple and natural living?"

"Unconscious imitation. A nervous businessman was part of the madness of a large city. Wishing a calmer environment, he moved to an unspoiled island in the tropics, inhabited by a few natives. But the businessman brought his nervous mind and manners with him. Believing that his agitation was a sign of normality, the natives eagerly imitated his jumpiness. After awhile, anyone who was not nervous was considered abnormal."

TRUE BENEFITS

"How can I attain my true benefits?"

"By discovering what they are."

"How is this accomplished?"

"By seeing quite clearly that your present benefits can't keep you from crying."

TEACHINGS

"Who are these teachings for?"

"For whoever knows that he does not know, for whoever is secretly tired and perplexed, for whoever wants to be who he really is."

"Then they are for me."

SUMMARY

"Your various summaries of the human situation have been very enlightening to us. May we have another one?"

"Whether you are aware of it or not, you have chosen a certain way of life for yourself. You must therefore reap the results of that choice. If you wish to choose another way, you are free to do so, after which different results will appear."

A MAN WHO HAS DARED

"Please tell us something about a man who is truly awakened."

"Outwardly he may appear quite usual, but inwardly he is a sun for a dark world. He is a man who has dared to plunge all the way into himself until seeing things as they are in reality. He knows much more about everyone than he can tell, for few people are able to take it. He exists only to those who can recognize him, to those who really want what he has to give."

HOW IT GOES

"How does it go?"

"A sincere student of the higher life came across a book of truth. His first reading aroused apprehension, for the book challenged his false assumptions. The second reading aroused interest, for something hard in him was beginning to melt. The third reading aroused inspiration, for he knew he had found a pure guide. The fourth reading aroused self-transformation, for printed truth blended with inner truth. That is how it goes."

THE WHOLE POINT!

"I wish to get to the point."

"There exists another state of life for you which is totally different from your present state. That is the whole point."

OBEDIENCE

"Religion stresses the need for obedience, which has always bothered me. Maybe it associates with my past in which I had to obey tyrannical authorities."

"Be cheerful about it. The problem will vanish once you grasp a certain fact. You must be obedient only to yourself, to your true and fundamental nature. That is the same as obedience to God and truth."

"I would have walked fifty miles in a storm to hear that single refreshment."

SUPPLY

"I am confused. Can you help me?"

"Yes."

"Then please give me what I want."

"I cannot supply what you want."

"But you said you could help."

"Ask me to supply what you need."

THE RULES OF THE GAME

"We are caught in our own trap!"

"Of course. Imagine yourself compelled to play a new kind of football game having numerous and complicated rules. The rules are so vague and contradictory you cannot even begin to understand and follow them. But in spite of that you are ordered to play the game, and when failing to play properly, you are punished! So man is caught in his own game, a game he neither comprehends nor controls. The game can never be anything but maddening, for its rules are based on illusions and on concealed self-interest. Liberty dawns for the man who finally sees that he himself contributes to the riotous game.''

THE FEARFUL MAN

''I am guilty of many cruel acts. I am ashamed of myself. I am secretly hostile toward truth. I am afraid I won't make it.''

''I have good news for you.''

HEAR THE TRUTH

''Am I capable of finding myself?''

''Are you capable of hearing truth without resenting it?''

''I don't know.''

''Then you will resent truth. However, all is not lost. Hear the truth *while* resenting it, but make up your mind to have nothing more to do with self-destructive resentment.''

''Part of me knows that this is the only sensible course.''

SEARCH FOR GOLD

''Something holds me back from seeking the way out, but I have no idea what it is.''

''Two friends were disappointed with their lives. Also, they feared additional disappointment. They became interested in searching for gold in a nearby mountain, so they read many books and studied maps. But on the day they were to head for the mountain, only one of them departed from home. This adventurous man had won a fine inner victory. He had determined to not let fear of disappointment block his search for gold.''

PROFITABLE QUESTIONS

''Suppose a person wishes to ask only profitable questions. What must he do?''

''Ask all questions in a right spirit.''

USE YOUR ENERGY!

"All this seems to call for more energy than we may have."

Pour every ounce of energy you have into your learning. Have no fear of spending it lavishly. That does not diminish energy, in fact, spending creates more. Picking a plum from a tree does not decrease the plum-producing power of that tree."

TWO DIRECTIONS

"Quite often we fail to benefit from the truth. Why?"

"A cosmic fact offered to a man can be turned into one of two directions. It can be turned by the man himself into a gain or a loss. It is like tossing an apple to a hungry but confused man. Unless he recognizes the object as an apple he is likely to let it drop to the ground."

"As you said last week, recognition is everything."

THE MISTAKEN MAP

"I am trying to reach Happy Hills."

"But you are on the road to the Valley of Despair."

"But my map says this is the road to Happy Hills."

"You need a thousand times more courage than you have."

"To do what?"

"To tear up the map."

SELF-REFERENCE

"We are told to abandon self-reference. I am not sure what it means."

"The false self imagines it is the center of the universe. A man lost a small coin in the street, which he mentioned to a passing policeman. A short time later some workers arrived with their heavy equipment and began tearing up the street to make room for new water pipes. Looking pleased, the man thanked the policeman for his all-out assistance. That is self-reference."

MEN WHO KNEW

"May we hear the names of men who really knew?"

"Jesus and Buddha head the list. There are many others with varying degrees of cosmic consciousness, including Lao-tse, Plotinus, Saadi, Shankara, Pythagoras, Socrates, Plato, Al-Ghazzali, Epictetus, Chuang-tse. You can add Marcus Aurelius, Baruch Spinoza, William Law, Blaise Pascal, Leo Tolstoy, Arthur Schopenhauer, Ralph Waldo Emerson."

"Thank heaven for the few who broke through."

ANGER

"Everyone is angry in one way or another, which is obviously self-destructive. How do these teachings help an angry person?"

"He comes to these teachings with his suppressed anger. After awhile it appears that he is becoming less angry, but this is just a new role he is playing unconsciously—the role of being a non-angry person. Then through self-work he becomes openly angry to himself, that is, he becomes aware of how angry he always was. Now he is truly departing from anger."

SWISS GIRL

"Speaking in general, what bothers us?"

"What bothers us is where we are *not*. It is like the Swiss girl who was employed at a French seaside village having a lively tourist trade. Homesick, she told the other girls about it. They reminded her of the pleasant surroundings and her good wages. She replied that her present location was beside the point. What bothered her, she said, was where she was *not*. We belong in a place other than the foreign psychic country we now inhabit."

THE PRICE

"What is the price of this book of real knowledge?"

"How many times a day do you get upset?"

"Five or six times."

"To you it is worth any price."

PERSONAL MIRACLE

"I have everything I need and yet have nothing I need. Do you understand my difficulty?"

"What you need is a personal miracle. Risk losing what you *call* yourself and that miracle will happen."

PERPLEXITY

"How did we get into this mess in the first place?"

"A child was told by several adults to be good. Observing the behavior of the adults, he concluded that goodness consisted of envy, sarcasm, and trickery. Years later, as an adult himself, he was resentful and greatly perplexed. He wondered why a person as good as himself should attract so much unhappiness."

"That is a perfect summary of how we go wrong."

DIFFERENT WORLD

"I am afraid I won't succeed in my attempts to become someone."

"You don't have to succeed at all. If you could see the full meaning of this you would live in a different world."

METEORITES

"What prevents the saving truth from reaching man?"

"Nothing but man's own resistance. Meteors provide the perfect illustration. Astronomers tell us that millions of meteors hurtle into the earth's atmosphere every day. Only a few succeed in penetrating this outer zone to land on earth. The rest are burned up by the atmosphere. The successful ones are called meteorites. Man surrounds himself with a psychological atmosphere of resistance and negativity, thus preventing truth from reaching his innermost being. But the individual who welcomes a mental meteorite will feel a wonderful impact."

WHY

"Why is this way better than my usual way?"
"Why is freedom better than imprisonment?"

ACCEPT YOURSELF

"I wish I could accept myself as my own rescue."
"Just do so. Imagine a factory producing a wide variety of industrial products. Its manager sees a need for newness in the factory, so he uses the factory's own products to build a new and modern factory. Man has no idea of the marvels of himself. He is capable of starting right where he is to build a totally new nature."

OUTSTANDING POINTS FROM CHAPTER 1

1. Stand in the right position to receive new truths.
2. Give full attention to your inner adventure.
3. What you really need is your own liberated nature.
4. These teachings are the only real fun on earth.
5. Attain true benefits by seeing what they really are.
6. These ideas are for those who sincerely want out.
7. The whole point is that another life exists for you.
8. You are now on the truly sensible course in life.
9. Learn to recognize cosmic facts when they appear.
10. You can witness the personal miracle of self-change.

Chapter 2

HOW TO PERFORM ENRICHING ACTIONS

AWAKENED CENTER

"It has been said that a certain small center within us knows the truth, even when our other parts remain asleep. If only we could build this awakened center."

"That is the whole idea. This right center resembles a man standing on a foggy hilltop at dawn. As the rising sun slowly dissolves the fog the man is able at first to sight nearby rocks and bushes. With more sunlight he sights distant trees and slopes. As the sun continues to rise he recognizes more and more of his surroundings, whichever way he turns. Build your awakened center with daily action."

WALLS

"What prevents me from seeing what I must see?"

"Certain walls in your mind."

"But I am unaware of such walls."

"That is why they remain."

"How can I tear down the walls?"

"By not fighting when reality tries to tear them down."

"For years I have sensed the wrongness of my fighting."

THE NEXT STEP

"I don't know the next step toward the way out."

"There is always a next step. Remember that. Switch

from self-condemnation to self-understanding. Do not put up with a wandering mind. Become aware of mechanical reactions. Never enjoy self-pity. Do not be deceived by society's lofty but empty speeches. See that self-insight and self-change are the same thing. These are superb next steps. Find more for yourself.''

WRONG QUESTIONS

''Why do teachers decline to answer certain questions?''

''Often because the question has no reality in it. Hypnotized human beings wrongly assume their questions are perfectly logical and intelligent, never realizing that a faulty machine can only give out faulty products. For instance, a man might ask how to achieve worldly success. That is a wrong question. If that man became king of the world he would still be a slave to his own negative nature.''

TRUE INDIVIDUALITY

''How can we work for our real benefits?''

''Imagine yourself standing in the middle of a stream. The flowing water tends to push you downstream. If you give in to the pressure you do what most people do, that is, you permit yourself to be carried downstream. You must be truly individualistic. You must not let a negative self or a negative society carry you away. Instead, go against the common social flow and work your way upstream. There are astonishing sights at the source of the stream.''

THE CHANCE

''Who has a chance to wake up?''

''Whoever gives himself the chance.''

BE TEACHABLE

''How can we end self-defeating attitudes toward the truth?''

''The next time you attend a truth-lecture observe the attitudes and words and facial expressions of the other listeners. Observe that man who is actually boasting about his weaknesses. See that woman whose face barely hides her fear and hostility toward the truth. Notice that person who is confused about the lecture, but who still makes an honest effort to understand. Now observe yourself. What are your attitudes? Be a teachable listener.''

PERSONAL HEALING

''It takes courage to speak the truth about the terrible human condition.''

''It takes even more courage to speak the truth about one's inner and personal condition, but that is what heals the condition.''

''May we discuss the details of this topic in a future class?''

THE BANK

''Why do these teachings emphasize individual contemplation instead of attendance at religious or philosophical meetings?''

''Because a poor man in a bank is still a poor man.''

''So private contemplation is the sure way to inner wealth?''

''Yes, and in that case a man's insight is tremendous. He knows at a glance whether the religious bank has real or counterfeit money.''

PEACH TREE

''It seems that we are absent when we should be present.''

''Right. It can be illustrated by a young man who is given a fruitful peach tree by his father. The boy is told he must care for the tree, after which he can sell the peaches and keep the profit. But when the peaches ripen the boy is carelessly wandering around the noisy city, so the fruit is stolen by passing birds. Only as we value our lessons by remaining close to them can we collect the inner reward.''

MAGIC MOMENT!

"What happens when an unaware person hears these facts for the first time?"

"Something hits him but he doesn't know what. He is like a desert fox struck by rain for the first time. The newness of truth is so startling he has no idea how he should react. *This split second of suspended judgment is his great opportunity to change himself.* Unfortunately, most hearers miss the magic moment. They instantly spill out with habitual and mechanical reactions that fill the empty palace with junk. They argue or reject or feel threatened or want to run away. Be different. Leave the mental palace empty. Watch what happens."

CHALLENGE

"I feel challenged on every side."

"Challenge your own misconceptions about life. Remain brave and steadfast when this challenge produces unexpected and uncomfortable results."

"But my challenges come from the outside."

"Never. They come from your own misconceptions. Follow my counsel and you will see that the inner and outer are the same, which frees you from challenges."

HOW TO BEGIN

"How can I begin to wake up?"

"Watch yourself in daily action. Just quietly observe whatever you do, say, think, feel. Neither condemn nor approve what you see, but simply look at it without judgment. Mentally stand back a short distance from yourself and look at your daily actions, just as if you were casually observing a stranger. One result will be the faint feeling that you are not at all the person you have taken yourself to be. This is the start of a fantastic adventure, and the beginning of a totally new life."

INCENTIVE

"I need an incentive for not going along with the crowd."

"Observe the hysterical stampede of the crowd."

"Incentive enough."

TAKE THE DIRECT ROUTE

"I wish to increase the efficiency of my inner work."

"Then take the direct route. A businessman enjoyed working in his home garden, and when doing so was only a few yards from his phone. But there was no nearby door, so when the phone rang he had to rush around to a side door. After installing a door next to the garden he took the direct route. I will tell you about three direct routes. Instead of secretly enjoying conflict, give up its false pleasure. Rather than sacrifice yourself to others, live your own life. In place of blaming others for your unhappiness, see the cause within yourself."

SELF-HARMING ACTIONS

"What about someone who complains that circumstances and other people are out to hurt him?"

"If he wants to stop getting hurt he must stop blaming anything and anyone outside of himself. He may not understand this at first, but it must be done."

"What must he do?"

"He must learn to recognize self-harming actions when he performs them. For example, he must not take pleasure in dominating others, and he must not sacrifice his mental integrity in order to gain material benefits."

GOAL AND REWARD

"What is my goal?"

"To find yourself."

"What is my reward?"

"To be yourself."

EARNING A LIVING

"Suppose I earn my living by selling something, perhaps foods. Is it possible to conduct business in this hysterical world while remaining calm and relaxed?"

"Certainly, if you have dissolved the illusion of having a separate self. It is this fictitious person who demands control over events, who argues, agonizes, and worries over competition. When the false self goes, so do all troubles go, for then you are One with the Cosmic Whole. Because you are unconcerned with results, you earn either a poor or rich living, but you are a free, sane, and happy human being."

ENTER THE WATER

"Would it not be wise for me to remain at a distance from these ideas until I understand them better?"

"There was once a man who declared he would not enter the water until he had learned how to swim."

REFUSE TO COMPROMISE

"It seems that compromise is half our problem."

"A group of people were told about a rare fruit having a uniquely delicious taste. Wishing to possess this new fruit, the group visited various orchards to request it. The orchardists had no knowledge of the fruit, but still tried to make a profit by offering familiar fruits as substitutes. Most people lazily accepted the substitutes. But one energetic woman refused to compromise. She continued her search until finding the rare fruit in an obscure orchard which few people ever visited."

"That is our mistake—we rarely venture beyond ourselves."

ACTION FOR SELF-RESCUE

"You say we can use discomfort for self-rescue. How?"

"Take any audience. Ask everyone who knows the difference between right and wrong to raise his hand. You will make everyone uncomfortable. Why? Because everyone feels trapped. Every man pretends and assumes he knows the difference between right and wrong, but his feelings tell a different story. Slumbering man is so sure he understands right and wrong, truth and falsehood, that he never even thinks about it. So this jolting test can be helpful to those who want to stop suffering from themselves, for they can now question their misleading assumptions.''

THE RIGHT PLACE!

''I wish to study cosmic science. Have I come to the right place?''

''Why do you wish to study?''

''Not to win public applause for my learning, but to straighten out my life.''

''You have come to the right place.''

SOMETHING TO THINK ABOUT

''Give us something to think about.''

''It is really astonishing. A man will spend years studying and working on his business or employment, making it successful and efficient. Yet he will not spend five minutes studying the greatest business of all—his own life here on earth.''

''You once explained this baffling behavior of man. You said that he rarely studies himself because he lives under the terrible illusion that he already knows what his life is all about. He trembles, fights, flees—and still insists he has self-command!''

TOY AND BOOK

''How can we outgrow useless and unnecessary involvements?''

''A Dutch artist once painted a picture of a boy turning away from a dropped toy because a book on a table had attracted his interest. The artist was teaching how our childish toys fall away by themselves as we catch a glimpse of something higher.''

CONGRATULATIONS

''Your teachings first disturb and then please me.''

''Congratulations. That is the right order. The disturbance is caused by truth challenging falsehood. You are then pleased by sensing the healthy necessity of this. A person who is first pleased and then disturbed is getting false teachings. He is pleased at hearing what he prefers to hear, after which he becomes disturbed by realizing he is still the same miserable person.''

UNIQUE PROCEDURE

''In what way is this procedure unique?''

''It begins by making you do things you don't want to do, such as seeing your real motives and going against hardened beliefs. It ends by letting you do whatever you want to do, for then you will never do anything harmful to yourself or others.''

DREAMING DRIFTERS

''You teach that right sight supplies right action. That is still unclear to me.''

''You sail your boat down the stream. You sight an underground rock. That sight makes you guide the boat right. Do you know why most people bump one rock after another? Because they are asleep in the boat, dreaming they are in command.''

INTELLIGENT ACTION

''Will you please review what is meant by intelligent action?''

''A man will ask for help in repairing his car or television set, but will he act as intelligently when his life needs repair? Rarely. Vanity refuses to admit the need for help. So vanity itself prevents the intelligent action by which he could escape psychic prison. The key to the cell is called *receptivity.*"

"One fact is clear. We cannot afford vanity."

AUTHENTICITY

"I want the authentic."

"Excellent. One speck of authenticity has more weight than a mountain of artificiality."

ELEVATION

"How does spiritual elevation proceed?"

"First you suffer from many things but do not know why. Then you suspect yourself as the cause of your troubles but are reluctant to admit it. Then you see how your unconscious cause produced the unhappy effect. Then you rise above cause and effect to the clear sky of awareness and peace."

THE FOURTH MAN

"We are so easily distracted from our search!"

"Lost in a jungle, four men decided to build one-man rafts for floating downstream to civilization. They began to search for suitable wood for the rafts. But one man, having heard rumors of buried treasure in the region, was soon looking for gold instead of wood. A second man also stopped his search for wood, for he foolishly believed that rescue would appear miraculously. The third man also stopped, preferring to spend his time in complaining and worrying. Only the fourth man kept to his aim. He built a raft which carried him to safety."

THE HEALING OF HUMILIATION

"Why are we here in this class?"

"To understand the invisible process by which our nature works. This insight enables us to let go, to permit the process to heal everything naturally."

"My friend left me. Can that ache be healed?"

"When he or she left you suffered from loneliness and humiliation. Examine the invisible process. See that it is your thought about the event that suffers, not your real nature. The authentic self cannot suffer from anything. Insight into the healing process is the very healing itself."

RIGHT ACTION

"Sometimes I feel unwanted. What should I do?"

"Nothing."

"Why do nothing?"

"Because usual actions, such as seeking new friends, separate you from the feeling, and separation prevents insight. Can you even understand a torn coat while walking away from it? Habitual actions only suppress the feeling for a short time. Have you ever noticed the slight depression that appears when the merry party ends?"

"But what is right action?"

"Total understanding is right action in itself."

THE LETTER

"How can we give these facts the higher value they deserve?"

"Ask more questions, then value the answers. A teacher held a letter before his students, then asked them to estimate its value. When the students replied that the letter was of little worth, the teacher urged them to ask questions about it, which they did. The letter became valuable to the pupils when learning it had been written by America's honored poet, Henry Wadsworth Longfellow."

LEARNING

"Starting today, I wish to find the way out."

"Then learn how to learn."

"I already know that."

"No, you know how to read and speak and think in a familiar way. Learning is quite another process."

"What is it?"

"Studying with a preference for the new and unfamiliar over the old and comfortable."

HOW TO LIVE CREATIVELY

"Please discuss creative living."

"It is living with a free mind and spirit. Creativity appears of itself with the ending of wasteful practices. Life constantly renews itself, providing rich supplies every moment, but they are wasted. It is like a hungry man who takes one bite of dinner and throws the rest away. Look at all the energy wasted in petty annoyance. That energy could be used to win self-insight."

"Creativity appears of itself with the ending of waste. That is a new thought for me."

CROSS OVER

"I cannot seem to cross over to the new land."

"Picture a boundary line which keeps you out of a wealthy country. The boundary consists of a fence and a ditch. If the fence is removed, is the boundary as formidable as before?"

"No."

"If the ditch is filled in, is the line erased completely?"

"Yes."

"If you still could not cross, it would be because the boundary still exists in your mind. I inform you that the fence and ditch to the new land are no longer there. Cross over."

HOW TO WIN

"No matter what I do I seem to lose."

"As long as you crave to win you will lose, even if you win. When you are consciously indifferent over winning or losing, you win."

ONE RIGHT ACT

"My complicated life overwhelms me."

"Do one right act. Make it as small as you like, but

do one right act. You have heard of many right acts in this class. For instance, freely concede that you really do not understand yourself. Or, be aware of your resistance to new ideas. These are powerful right acts. Remember, rightness alone can overwhelm wrongness. All this is much simpler than you imagine. Just perform one right act every day. Watch what happens.''

HOW TO FIND A TRUE TEACHER

''What does a confused seeker need to know?''

''There are two main difficulties in finding the way out, but both can be overcome. The first is the rarity of a teacher who really knows the answers. The second is the inability and the unwillingness of a seeker to recognize a true teacher should they meet. A sheep cannot recognize an eagle. So fearing destruction of his false values at the hands of a teacher, the seeker rejects the very truth that could heal him. But if the seeker's pain becomes unbearable enough, one small and honest part of him can guide him to a teacher and make him receptive to the offered truth.''

WHAT TO DO

''What must I do?''

''You must love your liberation more than you love to criticize.''

''You always get right to the point! I know there is no other way to make it.''

GARNETS

''Why do we fail to possess available truth?''

''Imagine someone eager to search some rocky hills for semiprecious stones, the garnet in particular. But he is so eager to search the area he fails to prepare his mind. He arrives at the hills without knowledge of the nature of garnets. His shovel brings up a pile of rocks and earth, which includes a valuable garnet. But unable to recognize a garnet, he walks away from it. A preliminary task of every seeker is to prepare his mind for recognition of the truth when it is unearthed.''

THE WISH

''I wish to be free.''
''Innocence is free.''

SWIFT TRAVELING

''How can we travel more swiftly?''

''Two Arab merchants left their homes on the same day to make separate journeys by camel to a distant city. One arrived several days earlier than the other. The slower merchant asked the speedy Arab for his secret. The swift traveler replied that he had traveled at night as much as he could, as well as day. The swift psychic traveler is one who has learned to use dark experiences for progress.''

NATURAL AGREEMENT

''Last week you used the phrase *natural agreement*. May I know its meaning?''

''Nothing is true unless a certain and deep part of your own nature agrees with it. Go by this rule and you will never go wrong. Someday you will see that a certain small part of you was right after all.''

''That small part of me feels the rightness of your words.''

HOPE

''I have lost all hope.''
''What a great accomplishment!''
''Accomplishment?''
''Have you ever noticed the pain in hope?''

ANOTHER WAY TO PROCEED!

''Why is it so hard to judge between the true and the false?''

''Because you assume that whatever arouses a thrilling

feeling is true, and whatever evokes an unpleasant emotion is false. That is how you wrongly meet every experience, that is how you live your entire life. What kind of life is it?''

''But how else can we proceed?''

''You can see that the truth that makes you free is above the present process which has made your life the secret terror that it is.''

LOOK CLOSELY

''Why do people refuse the gold of truth?''
''Because they think they already have it.''
''But surely their inner poverty is clear to them.''
''They claim that stone is gold and that gold is stone.''
''Can something be done for them?''
''Yes, if they will look closely at what they call gold.''

IN THE COLISEUM

''I have just read an interesting story that illustrates what we must do. The story was about Marcus Aurelius, the adopted son of a Roman emperor. As a young man, Marcus was taken to the coliseum to watch the battling gladiators. But while the crowd shouted at the violence below, Marcus sat quietly in the royal box and read a book of philosophy. Later, when becoming emperor of Rome, he set down his philosophical discoveries in a book of meditations.''

''Yes, the story has many lessons. For one, we must stand aside from human uproars to reflect upon the meaning of our lives here on this planet.''

INVOLVEMENT

''I am a very active person, involved in many groups and programs. In spite of everything I still feel empty and bored. Why?''

''Because you cannot get rid of thirst by running alongside the river.''

"How do I drink?"

"Did it ever occur to you to get involved in your own deliverance?"

TURNING POINT

"What can bring about a turning point in someone?"

"Seeing the vanity, the folly, and the uselessness of trying to cure another before curing oneself."

"Quite obviously there is no other way to contribute to social sanity."

SPIRITUAL SUPPLIES

"We need to make more use of the simple, everyday virtues."

"An Australian decided to search for gold in the deserts of his country. Loading the necessary tools and supplies on his back he set out on foot. After a few hours in the intense heat he dropped some of his supplies, and later dropped some more. He finally found gold, but was now without the needed equipment for making it his own. After recovering his supplies he had his gold. A man seeking spiritual gold must possess a full supply of the needed equipment, including self-honesty and self-reliance. We sense their necessity, don't we?"

YEARNING

"Why should I change myself?"

"Because at least a dozen times a day you yearn to do so."

PRIVATE LIVES

"It seems so important to become a successful person in the eyes of other people."

"Who told you it was important?"

"Many people, in one way or another."

"What are their lives like?"

"Pardon?"

"How do they live? Take a look at their private lives. How many are fearful, nervous, hostile, foolish, weak? And you listen to *them?* You let *them* tell you what is important? Incredible. When will you listen to your own nature?"

HUSBAND AND WIFE

"My wife and I intend to work together on these principles."

"That can lead to either swift advancement up the mountain or it can lead to the desert. If you use each other as allies in battling unwanted facts, it is tragic. But it will be extremely beneficial if you help each other to be more sincere and more receptive in the face of truth's challenges."

"Thank you for that explanation. It will keep us alert."

NEW LANGUAGE

"We wish to do whatever is necessary, so what is required?"

"A king of ancient Saxony invited some young men from other countries to become members of his royal guard. It was a high honor, and one requiring applicants to learn the language of Saxony. Those who succeeded became royal guards. There is a similar requirement for admittance into cosmic royalty. One must learn the lofty language of esotericism, which makes everything clear. It can be felt as well as heard. Your attendance in this class is teaching you this new language."

FACTS TO REMEMBER FROM THIS CHAPTER

1. Perform small but definite acts for self-newness.
2. Suspended judgment is a magic moment for you.
3. You are now in the right place for vast victories.
4. Realize that truth disturbs in order to cure.
5. It is intelligent action to request guidance.
6. Give these facts the higher value they deserve.

7. Erase the needless boundaries in your mind.
8. A true teacher appears to a true seeker.
9. Cherish self-liberation above all else.
10 Learn the cosmic language which tells of healing.

Chapter 3

HELP AND GUIDANCE TOWARD THE WAY OUT

REQUEST FOR HELP

"I have heard that a sincere request for help attracts help. True?"

"True. An innocent man was imprisoned by an evil prince. Escape seemed impossible. But upon noticing a small stream running outside his barred window, a plan for escape formed in the prisoner's mind. Writing a note requesting help, he placed it inside a walnut shell and tossed the sealed shell into the stream. He tossed a new walnut and note into the stream every day for many days. Nothing happened for awhile, but finally his cell door opened, making him a free man. A good prince had found one of his notes, and had sent a rescue party."

TWO TEACHERS

"Please tell us about different kinds of teachers."

"A teacher who speaks to your mind can give you needed knowledge, but to acquire a wholeness which is more than knowledge you need a much higher teacher. You need a whole man who can speak to the whole man in you. You can *feel* the truth of his message. The first teacher describes a peach tree. The second teacher helps you to taste a peach for yourself."

QUALIFICATION

"It seems necessary to qualify ourselves for help. How?"

"Accept advice as eagerly as you ask for it."

HOW TO ESCAPE THE STORM

"Why do people fail to find themselves?"

"Because, strangely, one of the most helpful questions you can ever ask a man is the very question which frightens him the most. It is to ask him what he is really like inwardly. Few people are even willing to hear the question to say nothing of answering it. Do you see the urgency of self-facing?"

"Yes, and I am encouraged by knowing about it. The only way to escape the storm is to understand its nature."

ACCURATE DIRECTIONS

"I need to hear accurate directions."

"They can be supplied by the truth within you, for truth speaks a language which is natural to your real self. A girl of ten was traveling with her American parents through a large foreign city. Becoming separated from her parents in the crowded streets, she lost her sense of direction. Remaining calm she stood on a corner and listened to the speech of various passers-by. Hearing a woman speak English, the girl asked the woman for directions to the hotel, which were supplied. The girl was soon reunited with her parents. Listen for your own natural directions."

HOW TO CORRECT OUTLOOKS

"Please give us help in correcting our outlooks."

"You view a certain situation. Ask yourself whose mental eyes see it, and you will reply that it is your mental eyes. But what is the origin of the outlook? It is your own past experiences and conditionings, both painful and pleasant. But you are not your habitual outlook any more than you are a pair of glasses you once wore. See through the eyes of Truth."

OPINIONS

"I am beginning to see how I cling to my opinions,

even when sensing how wrong they are. Why this fierce clinging?''

''You must realize that you are not your opinions or theories. An opinion is acquired accidentally, like picking up one leaf out of hundreds on the ground. But you gradually identify with it, that is, you think it tells you who you are. So you label yourself a member of Group X or Organization Z. Now you fear losing this mere label for you think it means the loss of your self. But you are not a label or an opinion. You are much more.''

RIGHT STATE

''Can constant association with the facts help us?''

''Can mere association with food end your hunger?''

''Obviously, we must be in a right mental state.''

''Association plus acceptance is the right state.''

USE ESOTERIC PRINCIPLES

''From your observation of me, what holds me back?''

''You have too much to do with others and too little to do with yourself. I will show you how to correct this. Never apologize to others by word or manner for any weakness you may have. In almost every case they will use it for their own ego-gratification. Instead, use esoteric principles to understand and end your weakness.''

''You seem to know my wants better than I do. What do I really want?''

''To get your life back.''

UPWARD CLIMB

''Give us something to assist our upward climb.''

''India has a mountain with a particular weather condition. A fog belt runs along the side of the mountain, but there is clear weather both on its top and at its base. So a climber wishing to reach the peak must enter the fog and come out on the upper side. I will give you an encouragement. Have no fear of entering psychological fog. Regardless of how it appears, it is an upward step.''

ON YOUR SIDE!

"We need to realize so many things."

"There is one realization, which if attained, leads you straight to a thousand psychic gems."

"You make us eager to know what it is!"

"Realize that the truth is on your side. No, you don't realize this as yet, for you still resist its healing message. Realizing that the truth is on your side is like opening a letter while expecting bad news, but finding an invitation to a banquet. Now, what must you live by?"

"By the fact that the truth is on our side."

OPPORTUNITY

"You once said that meeting an awakened man is both an opportunity and a crisis. I would like to hear more about that."

"An awakened man sees straight through other people, perceiving their actual natures and their concealed motives. This is terrifying to those who love self-deception, but a ray of light to anyone who no longer wants to suffer from himself."

THE GAP

"What determines whether we learn or not?"

"Someone who comes to a truth-class for the first time has a certain opportunity to learn. The truth will be quite different from what he expected it to be, that is, a wide gap will exist between his expectation and his hearing. Everything depends upon his attitude and action toward this gap. If in irritation or discomfort he closes the gap by returning to his original expectations and beliefs, he learns nothing. But if with genuine interest and earnestness he explores the meaning of this gap he has a chance to learn the secrets of life."

TRUE BOOK

"How can I tell whether or not I am reading a true book?"

"By having something true in you before reading the book."

"How can I gain this trueness?"

"By wishing for a book that speaks not to your fantasies but to *you*."

THE LESSON

"Inform us of something we must guard against."

"The poet Dante once set up his art equipment to paint an angel. His plans were interrupted by the unexpected appearance of some publicly prominent visitors. The lesson is, guard against interruptions of your inner artistry."

"In other words, maintain mental integrity."

WINGS

"I worry lest my human and financial supports should fail."

"Does a bird worry when a branch collapses under his feet? Not at all. He has wings. Develop your cosmic wings."

PLEASE YOUR TRUE NATURE

"I may not show it on the surface, but I am tired of living my life to please others."

"There is a way out, but diligence is required of you."

"Anything is better than the way I now sacrifice myself to others by trying to please them."

"Instead of trying to please others, please your own true nature. Just try it. Then, because your real nature is pleased with you, it will show you how to live rightly with others."

BUCKETS

"We seem unable to take what could be ours."

"Like a thirsty man walking in the rain without a bucket. In this group we are learning to make buckets."

SOURCE OF LIGHT

"It took several years, but I finally saw that I had been seeking answers in the wrong places."

"A teacher of esotericism wished to illustrate a certain principle to some new students. He gave two of them un-lighted candles, then asked one of them to light his candle from the other's candle. It could not be done, of course, for both candles were unlighted. The teacher then explained that only an illuminated man or book can spread light to those who need it."

GOOD NEWS!

"Today, may we hear some good news?"

"Anything honest and accurate is good news. Here are four examples. An emerald temporarily lost among pebbles is still valuable. There is something to hear which is far superior to that which our weak parts prefer to hear. You can have as much rescue as you are willing to recognize as rescue. Command yourself and you command the world."

"That is enough good news for a month!"

UNCONSCIOUS HAUNTINGS

"It seems that we are unconscious of most of our haunt-ings."

"Correct. Take a particular haunting—the fear of being blamed. Have you ever quietly studied this haunting to see how often it appears? Have you ever noticed how it keeps you nervous and defensive? If you no longer want to suffer from the fear of being blamed, make it conscious."

DRIVING HOME

"At the end of your last lecture you advised everyone to listen to himself, not to his friends. What was meant?"

"A story will explain. Six friends attended a truth-lec-ture together. While driving home the conversation was dominated by the most neurotic and deceitful person in the group. In hostility and fear of the truth he had heard, he criticized the speaker and told many lies. This is a true story, and the way it often happens. I gave that advice because I did not want the darkness of one man to injure the seed of truth by which others could grow.''

WEEDS AND FLOWERS

''I am tired of being led astray by cunning deceivers.''

''Then stop consenting to it.''

''I am consenting to being deceived?''

''Of course you are. A person accepts weeds as flowers only when he has not learned the difference in the two. Your lack of discernment leads you into nervous consent. You close your eyes and accept weeds sprayed with cheap perfume. Open your eyes and see for yourself.''

''With the help of this group I will do just that.''

RIGHT TEACHER

''Who can teach me rightly?''

''Someone with no compulsion to teach.''

THE MOUNTAIN PASS

''Please discuss the value of self-questioning.''

''A scout for a party of Western pioneers was riding ahead of the wagons. Coming to the base of a mountain he looked around for a pass. Seeing none he persisted with a direct question to himself—he asked how he could get through. Before long he found the needed pass. The spiritual scout must ask himself the same question, persistently and earnestly. By asking how he can get through he will eventually find the pass.''

QUALITY AND QUANTITY

''In studying religious history I have noticed that the real teachers were never followed by the masses, at least not for long.''

''A real teacher is interested in the quality of his disciples, not in quantity. The larger the organization the less truth it possesses. Increased membership means more money, more power, more dependence upon each other in supporting false ideas. A real teacher has nothing to do with all this. He wishes to show the way out to the few who want out.''

CONSCIOUS BUSINESSMAN

''Can these teachings help a busy businessman to remain calm and efficient?''

''They help anyone, anywhere, but take a businessman who has seen the light. To all outward appearances he may seem to be all wrapped up in commercial competition, but the man himself knows better. While one part of him conducts business, another part remains in detached command of everything. These two parts are not really divided, for a conscious man possesses self-unity. The two parts simply work together, like two hands. Free from concern over results, the awakened businessman works calmly and efficiently at earning his living.''

PROCRASTINATION

''Once in awhile I talk with people about the importance of self-knowledge. Most are procrastinators. They say they will explore the inner world as soon as a few pressing problems are solved.''

''Procrastination is illogical from every viewpoint. It is like the man who wanted to cross the stream, so he sat on the bank to wait for all the water to run by.''

AN AWAKENED MAN

''If we were to meet an awakened man, could we recognize his superior state?''

''You cannot credit a man with more insight than you yourself possess. You cannot see above your own level. Only a man who knows silver can credit another man with possessing real silver. Insight alone recognizes insight. So an awakened man is never understood by sleeping men. His insight does not exist in their minds, therefore contact is impossible. You can now see why authentic teachers are mostly ignored or scorned. But all is well, for as you begin to awaken you can begin to recognize the few who offer authentic help.''

SELF

''I was once told to believe in myself. Is that possible?''

''Who is this self you speak about?''

''I don't know.''

''Then you must be careful to not quote popular sayings without understanding them. If by your self you mean all the accumulated illusions you have about yourself it would be dangerous to believe in that. But if you mean your true and original nature it is a magnificent act to accept that nature.''

''Thank you.''

WHAT BOTHERS PEOPLE

''The trouble is, we don't know what bothers us.''

''A husband and wife enjoyed nature hikes. They usually followed a trail that wandered through a short stretch of woods. One afternoon the same thought occurred to both of them. There was something unnatural about the woods they passed through so often. An investigation revealed what had bothered them. One large tree was foreign to the area; it did not belong there naturally. Apparently someone had transported and planted the strange tree many years earlier. You must see what is unnatural to you, such as strife and bitterness.''

ACCEPTANCE

''I wish to be accepted into your class.''

''You must qualify by being very tired of something.''

''Well, I am very tired of anxious self-defense.''

''Accepted.''

INSINCERE INQUIRERS

"I have seen many inquirers depart empty-handed from a real teacher. Why does this happen?"

"Because the inquirer is insincere, unready."

"Can the teacher recognize insincerity in an inquirer?"

"Instantly. The pretentious inquirer gives himself away in dozens of ways of which he is unaware. They include chattering instead of listening, a nervous need to interrupt, a veiled facial expression of contempt when told the truth, a wish to argue, an attempt to flatter the teacher."

SHOCK AND SUFFERING

"Please discuss the wise use of shock and suffering."

"Imagine yourself standing over the bed of a deeply sleeping friend. In a quiet voice you inform him that his dog is digging up and ruining his garden. You urge him to wake up and call off the dog. Will he hear you? Not at all. His sleep is too deep. That is man's psychic condition. He cannot even wake up when told it is for his own benefit to do so. Only a vigorous shaking will arouse him. Shock and suffering serve the purpose of awakening a sleeping man, *but he must use the shock to run out into the garden, not to resent whoever wakes him up.*"

GULLIBILITY

"I am afraid I am gullible. I will follow anything exciting or attractive all the way to the inevitable shock. What can I do?"

If a thousand people declare that a lemon is sweet, do you believe it?"

"No."

"Why not?"

"Because I know better from my own taste."

"Know that you can know everything from your own taste."

STUDY METHOD

"Please suggest a method for efficient study of these ideas."

"See how much attention you can give to one topic at a time. One day you might study the value of self-government. The next day you could examine the folly of living with automatic assumptions. In time you will see connections between ideas, for instance, you will see how independent thinking keeps you out of trouble in the first place. It is like studying an orange tree. By concentrating in turn on its fruit, its leaves, its roots, you see how they operate together to form the whole tree."

EXCITEMENT

"I have been to fifteen teachers and not one of them has helped me."

"Do you want help or do you want the excitement of meeting new teachers?"

"I see what you mean."

FAMILIAR MELODY

"The melody of truth sometimes seems absent."

"The truth is always sending out its melody. Listen. Hear. Recognize! A musician lived in some hills where a homeland army was resisting the invasion of a barbaric country. Realizing he was surrounded by both friend and foe, the musician acted to help his countrymen who lost their way during nighttime battles. Opening the windows, the musician sat at his piano and played over and over a melody familiar to his own people, but not known by the invaders. Hearing and recognizing the tune the lost soldiers followed it all the way to the musician and to help."

BENEFICIAL LOSS

"Some of the facts given in this class seem to threaten me with loss. I do not understand it but I do feel as if I might lose something."

"You *are* losing something, and should shout with joy over it. You still assume it is a loss of your self, when in fact it is a loss of the imaginary self which causes so much damage."

"This is a turning point for me."

"Yes, so make the most of it by losing the artificial self as soon as possible."

INVITE UNDERSTANDING!

"Can God be known?"

"Certainly. All you need do is to stop thinking about God."

"I fail to understand."

"God is not an *idea*. God as an idea produces thousands of gods, causing religious division and conflict, plus hypocrisy."

"But how can God be known?"

"In this class you will learn how to think when necessary, and how to be above habitual thought. When not in thought you know God by being in Oneness with the All. Have patience. You will understand. Invite understanding."

TRAVEL UPWARD

"Please give us whatever we need."

"You cannot explain with words those secrets which are above the level of words. Language is like the directory found on the first floor of a large office building. It can tell you what exists on the higher floors but it cannot carry you up there. After consulting the directory you must personally travel upward. So every seeker must be careful here. He must not mistake knowledge of spiritual words for an actual and personal uplifting experience."

SELF-DOUBT

"I am filled with self-doubt."

"Do not have the slightest hesitation in doubting everything you think and feel about yourself."

"But doubt makes me feel uncomfortable."

"The road to self-certainty leads straight through the jungle of self-doubt. Stay on the road, enduring everything, which is true heroism. Watch the eyes of people who pretend to be certain. Do you want to live in that kind of self-made misery?"

"Not any more."

DEMANDS AND RESULTS

"I wish to find the way out as swiftly as possible."

"Then no longer demand that results conform to your desires."

"But this is how I have always lived."

"Which is why you have always been frustrated and resentful."

"But why shouldn't results match my desires?"

"Why *should* they?"

"It is so hard to let go."

"Just let go. In spite of all your fear, nothing harmful can possibly happen to you."

INTENSITY

"I would like to increase my intensity toward the inner adventure."

"Your level of intensity will be matched exactly by your level of understanding. Now reverse that statement. Your understanding will be equaled by your intensity. What happens to the intensity of a medical scientist who senses he is finally on the right road to a new cure? It increases. Let more understanding arouse more intensity."

COSMIC GOAL

"Help us stick to our lofty aims."

"Imagine a party of explorers in unknown territory. They spend all their time avoiding the dangers of marshes and storms and wild animals. That is all they do—avoid dangers. Because of this they never set a goal of reaching the mountaintop from where they could view everything. That is man. He is so busy avoiding dangers to his faulty beliefs that he has no cosmic aim. Forget the so-called dangers. March toward your elevated view.''

WHAT MUST BE DONE

''Take anyone who has found the way out. What has he done that we have not done?''

''He has risked rejection, not once or twice, but hundreds of times. This shattered his old nature, which made room for the new.''

''And we have not risked rejection?''

''No. You huddle fearfully in a corner. Try to see that what you really fear is the loss of false ideas about yourself. Now, in order to get out, what must you do?''

''Risk rejection.''

HARBOR

''How can I reach harbor?''

''By realizing that you are completely lost at sea.''

''But I already know that.''

''No, you try to feel secure by imagining what the harbor looks like, or by picturing it as you would like it to be. You will reach harbor only when you have no preconceived ideas of what it looks like.''

AUTHENTIC ASSISTANCE

''Please comment on our search for authentic assistance.''

''It is certainly right to seek help from a man who knows, but to lean on him is to miss your opportunity. The difficulty is that most people are unaware of how dependency triumphs over learning. But the path starts at an earlier point than this. You cannot learn from a man who knows until your own inner exploration has shown you the difference between an authentic teacher and a dramatic charlatan.''

LET GO!

"I need to convince myself that my ideas about life are all wrong."

"You are already convinced by what happened to you in the last twenty-four hours. Now have the courage to let go."

USE A CRISIS

"We must remember our lessons!"

"True. One lesson is to use a crisis to gain more insight, instead of missing the opportunity. It can be illustrated by some Asian farmers who were trying to introduce several kinds of berries to their fields. A government expert urged them to visit an experimental farm where the berries were being grown successfully, but the farmers declined. A crisis developed when the fields failed to produce satisfactory berries. The farmers wisely permitted the crisis to teach its lesson. They visited the experimental farm where they learned how to grow tasty berries."

SELF-RESCUE

"We are told to place no mind above our own, but I am baffled. How can a confused self rescue the self?"

"You can put yourself into your own hands or into your own clutches, but you must know the difference in the two."

"I am here to learn just that."

REAL SUCCESS

"In one way or another, most of us feel like failures. Even when financially or socially successful, the feeling of failure continues to haunt."

"Forget about society's standards of success. They are miserable failures. Simply see that up to now you have failed to devote your life to inner awakening. Something can be done about this kind of failure. It can be changed into victory. This is real success."

REFRESHMENT

"You have helped me see quite clearly that the truth never fails to supply those who really want refreshment."

"Early settlers in South America were curious about a certain kind of palm tree found in dry regions. Wherever they found the tree they also found luxuriant vegetation growing beneath it. A study of the tree provided the answer. The tree had extraordinary power to draw moisture from the air, which it then sprinkled onto the ground below. Seeds and plants were attracted to the abundance of water. Like that tree, truth supplies an abundance to those who want and appreciate its refreshing offerings."

CHAPTER 3 IN HELPFUL SUMMARY

1. A sincere request attracts authentic aid.
2. You are now learning how to get your life back.
3. Powerful truth is always on your side.
4. Everything honest and accurate is good news.
5. Practice these principles in daily work.
6. Drop whatever is unnatural to your real self.
7. Find individual ways to invite more light.
8. Use rejection to end the fear of rejection.
9. Have the courage to let go of useless opinions.
10. Truth is always ready with abundant refreshment.

Chapter 4

REVEALED SECRETS ABOUT
HUMAN NATURE

TRACKS IN THE SNOW

"I would like to know what people are really like."

"An artist lived and painted in a mountain cabin. Every morning he found pleasure in studying the tracks in the snow left by animals passing in the night. At a glance he knew his cabin had been passed by a bear or fox or deer. You can be a psychic artist who knows a man's real nature at a glance. Every person leaves his tracks in the snow which can be observed and interpreted. For instance, those who dream of glory in tomorrow have not found themselves today. Also, a man with considerable self-hate will often play the role of a compassionate person."

ENDLESS DEMANDS

"I am pressured into doing burdensome things I really don't want to do. If I learn how to own my own life will I be free of the endless demands of others?"

"Of course. It is like owning your own home. You don't have to pay rent to others."

FREEDOM FROM ANGRY PEOPLE

"I am afraid of people. Will these facts help me, especially when others are angry toward me?"

"They turn anger into nothing. With persistent self-work there will be nothing in you which can be frightened, bluffed, shamed, intimidated or made to feel evil or inferior. You will simply stand there and see an angry man or woman as a pathetic and self-tormented human being.''

''That would certainly be a new kind of world for me.''

INCREDIBLE MAN

''Last week you said that man was an incredible being. What did you mean?''

''It is incredible that a man will live on earth for years without once asking why he is here. It is incredible that he will suffer terribly from himself without seeking the cause and cure. It is incredible that he will continue to build a kind of security which leaves him just as insecure as before. It is incredible that when given a rescuing fact he promptly twists it to fit his illusions.''

COSMIC VOYAGE

''How does cosmic science explain frantic fights among humans?''

''Mankind is like passengers on a ship pushing through a heavy fog. Fearful of the unknown ahead, the passengers fight each other for turns at the wheel, each falsely claiming to know the way to the safe harbor. After his frantic turn at the wheel a passenger huddles back in his cabin, hoping that the next man at the wheel is not also a bluffing charlatan. Everyone makes the same mistake. He tries to substitute his personal course for the cosmic voyage.''

JUDGMENT

''I have my own judgment.''

''Yes, but who is going to save you from it?''

VICTIMS

''For the last few days I have been thinking of how we are all the victims of each other.''

''A person failing to think from his cosmic mind is the ready victim of every other person who also fails to think for himself. People mistakenly assume that borrowed ideas can keep them safe. You might as well lock your house and leave the key hanging on the door.''

''What do you mean by a cosmic mind?''

''A mind which sees the whole of life, not just the personal part which an individual believes is the whole.''

EFFORTLESS GOODNESS

''I am baffled how people can perform a good act one minute but be unkind the next.''

''When wanting a reward a man can perform a good act without having a good nature. He is self-divided. His next act will be harmful. Only an undivided man is truly good. His actions will be motiveless and effortless. A flower easily gives out its perfume because it is a flower.''

IDLE CURIOSITY

''I wish to attend your esoteric class for the first time.''

''Welcome, but do not come out of idle curiosity.''

''If I observe idle curiosity in myself I will tell you about it at the second meeting.''

''If you come out of idle curiosity you will not come to the second meeting.''

CANDY

''I am beginning to see what you mean by artificial compassion. I have seen several instances of it in the last month.''

''Artificial compassion has its source in self-interest. It is like the boy who bought two candy bars, one for himself and one for his brother. On the way home he ate one of them. When reaching home he sadly told his brother of an unfortunate mistake that had happened—he had accidentally eaten his *brother's* candy.''

BIOGRAPHY

''Give us a brief biography of spiritual success.''

''No man ever found himself without first feeling he has

been a faker all his life. However, he did not then condemn himself, but sought the real beneath the fakery."

"Do you know what I like about these teachings? Every time they say that man has fallen into a pit they throw him a rope!"

STUDY FACIAL EXPRESSIONS

"Please give us a method for seeing people as they really are."

"Study facial expressions until you see beyond the masks and sense what people are really thinking. Deliberate practice at this will yield astonishing secrets. A frozen face means she is hiding something. Wandering eyes indicate disinterest. Mechanical enthusiasm indicates that depression will follow. A slight scowl means he sees no profit for himself. A fixed smile indicates tension. Expressing great concern means he is using your problem to forget his own."

CHANGE

"If I change but others don't, what good will it do?"
"It will do no good except to you."

DISAPPEARING ACT

"It is obvious that insight into negative people can keep us from troublesome involvements with them. May we have an example?"

"Notice how neurosis is always performing a disappearing act. An unhealthy person appears on the scene and in an attempt to gain personal advantages he does his usual damage. He then departs, disappears, leaving others to suffer from the damage. A person who has ruined his own life will have no conscience about ruining the lives of others. Let this insight keep you away from such deceitful people."

CONSCIENCE

"It has been said that only an awakened man has a conscience. In what way does his conscience operate?"

"He does not seek self-profit by taking advantage of human weaknesses."

SOCIETY'S GAME

"Why is it so difficult to stop playing society's foolish game?"

"Because you still desire the prizes of the game."

"How can I give them up?"

"By seeing how they injure you."

"And how can I see this?"

"You *feel* the injury every hour. See what you feel."

FRIENDLIEST ACT

"There is so much artificiality in social relationships I wonder whether real friendship exists at all."

"Only a real teacher is capable of real friendship, though few human beings are able to see it. The fact that a real teacher is not out to gain your friendship is the friendliest act on earth."

"Yes, I understand that. He has no need to exploit others in the name of friendship."

GREAT TEACHER

"If only a great teacher like Christ or Buddha would return to earth! How different it would be!"

"If he commanded you to abolish anger, would you do so?"

"Most certainly."

"Then why haven't you done so?"

THE SENTRY

"I am trying to understand the connection between my inner state and my relations with others."

"It is illustrated by a sentry who stands nighttime guard over his sleeping companions. By remaining awake and alert the sentry serves both himself and his friends, but if he falls asleep he invites disaster to both himself and the others. In the same way a man in psychic sleep is a danger to others because he is first a danger to himself. Or stated differently, the only man who serves others rightly is the man who also serves himself rightly.''

SEE THE DIFFERENCE!

''These teachings seem hard on people.''

''No, they are hard on the delusions which cause people to suffer. See the difference in this and you will not remain the kind of human being you now are.''

''The change would be most welcome.''

LIKE ATTRACTS LIKE

''Why do I attract the kind of people I do?''

''Because of the law of similar levels.''

''What does that mean?''

''It means you attract people dwelling on the same psychic level as you. Like attracts like.''

''How can I attract people on a higher level?''

''Raise your own level.''

''Where do I start?''

''Get tired of the punishments of your present level.''

STRANGE WORLD

''It is a strange world. We make the world what it is and then complain about it.''

''It is even stranger than that. The worst thing you can do to some people is to take away the cause of their beloved complaints.''

CORRECTIVE THINKING

''We are victims of our own wrong thinking. Please discuss it.''

''Wrong thinking is like a man who takes daily strolls while paying no attention to where he goes. He is shocked and saddened to find himself in endless trouble. One day he walks straight into a rioting mob, the next day he falls into a marsh, the third day he gets lost in the woods. His careless thinking takes him to these places but he fails to realize it. So pay attention to your thinking until seeing how it produces the kind of experiences you have. This is corrective thinking.''

HOW TO CHANGE YOUR WORLD

''I wish to change my world.''

''Discover what makes your world whatever it is.''

''Please help me do this.''

''From the day of your birth society imposed upon you its fixed description of the world. Society said it was a world where you must fight, where you must be liked and accepted, and so on. Through thought and speech and action you repeated this description until it hardened into the only world you knew. You were then stuck with this illusory and punishing world. *Cease to repeat the description.* That will make the false world fall away, to reveal the real.''

THE BOOK

''I sincerely seek help. Can you recommend a good book?''

''Yes. Try this one with the green cover.''

''Oh. Don't you have one with a blue cover?''

DISRESPECT

''I feel that I am not treated with enough respect.''

''You gain great pleasure at feeling disrespected, don't you?''

''That is not the point.''

''It is precisely the point. It takes a brave man to give up the self-destructive pleasure of feeling disrespected.''

''That is baffling, but I want to think about it.''

HIDDEN WATER

''What is the explanation of the success of those men and women who have found the way out?''

''They could not remain satisfied with society's shallow answers. This activated a feeling of urgency. The survival of a certain breed of zebra in the Namib Desert of Africa depended upon its ability to find water in dry lands. Over the centuries this sense of urgency developed new talents in the zebra. It is able to sniff through the sands to detect hidden pools of water below. The needed water is then reached by digging with tough hoofs. Similarly, an individual feeling the need for spiritual water can develop his powers for finding it.''

FREE OF THE FOX

''Why do I get into trouble with people?''

''Because you expect a fox to behave like a lamb.''

''What causes this mistake?''

''Your inability to really see the difference between a fox and a lamb.''

''What is my weakness?''

''Your desperate hope that he or she might behave less like a fox and more like a lamb. Give up illusory hope and see the fact about him or her, whatever it is. Only then will you be free of the fox.''

HOW TO UNDERSTAND PEOPLE

''Tell us about something we don't see but think we do.''

''One of man's greatest delusions is believing that he already understands himself. He then projects this false belief to assume he understands other people. This explains human collisions and griefs, which always start with self-deception. You understand others only by first understanding yourself.''

''That explains a thousand problems.''

COSMIC INSPIRATION

''Why are we so easily influenced by wrong people and wrong ideas?''

''A man can be influenced by wrongness only when there is something wrong in him.''

"How can he be influenced by rightness?"

"Rightness is not on the level of influence. Rightness resides on the loftier level of cosmic inspiration."

"You mean we must learn to be inspired, not influenced?"

"Yes. And a man can be inspired by rightness only when there is something right in him."

THE ROOT

"Why do we fail to find healing?"

"A large party of people suffering from dizziness appealed to a skilled physician for healing. He instructed them to dig up a certain root in the forest and make a healing brew from it. Some of the patients were too lazy to dig for the root. Others carelessly dug up the wrong root and then called the physician a faker. Others found the root, mixed it with some sugary but useless roots and made a commercial success out of the venture. Only one man obeyed instructions. He was restored to a clear mind."

TRUE GUIDES

"I have been given ten books of self-help. How can I tell which ones, if any, are true guides?"

"Go out into the world and carefully observe men and women as they really are. Look behind cunning masks to see concealed attitudes and motives. See the deceptiveness of people. Now go through the books. Those that agree with what you saw are the true guides."

THOSE WHO ARE READY!

"What kind of people are ready for this class?"

"First see the kind of people who are not ready. This class is not for those who believe they already have the answers, nor for those who wish to teach, rather than learn. It is not for those who still get an ego-thrill from arguing and scorning, either openly or silently. This class is for those who do not know the answers and have come to the honest point in their lives where they are ready to admit it. Such people can eventually know what life is all about."

GROCERIES

"I would like to attend your class."

"We meet Saturday at ten in the morning."

"I usually shop for groceries on Saturday morning, but maybe I can make it."

"You won't make it."

"How do you know?"

"You have just told me what you really value."

NATURAL WARMTH

"I spent yesterday evening with some relatives. They complained that their lives were cold and dreary. For the first time I saw them as lost human beings."

"People are like refrigerated flowers. Refrigeration preserves flowers but who wants to be a cold flower? People fight to preserve their frozen beliefs and then complain of the cold! Take an individual out of his psychic refrigeration and his natural warmth revives."

TWO KINDS OF SEEKERS

"Please comment on sincere and insincere seeking."

"It is no sign of sincerity or spirituality to turn toward heaven when things go wrong on earth. How quickly heaven loses out when earthly fortunes improve!"

"Still, troubled people need help."

"An insincere person with a problem seeks comfort and relief, which is definitely not the same as seeking the cause of the trouble—the person himself. This is why he endlessly repeats his pattern of having a crisis followed by a plea for help. A sincere seeker constantly acquires self-insight, crisis or not."

TOMORROW

"In order to hear your magnificent messages I will follow you around the world."

''Tomorrow we will see whether you will follow me across the street.''

THE WILD HORSE

''I have come to a definite conclusion about man-made systems which claim to help the individual. They merely offer different kinds of burdens.''

''A wild horse was lured into captivity by some merchants who seemed compassionate, for they gave the horse hay and water. But when the horse found himself with a load of bricks on his back he shook them off and ran away. But he was soon lured by other merchants who appeared kindly but who soon loaded him with bales of rice. Finally seeing what was happening, the horse ran away and never again associated with merchants.''

RIGHT VIEWPOINT

''What is the right viewpoint to have toward someone who is obviously evil and cruel?''

''See him as evil, also, see him as someone who suffers terribly from himself. But see him in both these ways at the same time. Seeing him only as evil may arouse a self-righteous sense of superiority in you. And seeing him just as someone who suffers from himself may activate egotistical sentimentality which is merely a cunning projection of your own self-pity. The right viewpoint is to see him without self-reference, for this tells the whole story about him.''

SELF-SUCCESS

''I feel I have failed other people.''

''Failing others and failing yourself are the same thing. Do you see what this means? It means it is useless to try to behave rightly toward others without first succeeding with yourself.''

''How we deceive ourselves! We claim to want self-success, but that is the last prize we pursue. Yes, I see your point. We think we can behave rightly toward others while continuing to act wrongly toward ourselves. It can't be done. Self-success is the same as other-success."

ELIGIBILITY

"What determines whether or not a teacher admits an applicant to a class of higher knowledge?"

"No teacher ever really accepts or rejects an applicant. The person's own level of psychic maturity or immaturity determines his eligibility."

PARROTLAND

"You say we must see beyond ordinary life. What is meant?"

"In Parrotland there once lived a certain parrot who succeeded in becoming an admired Important Parrot. One day on a trip he lost his way to stray beyond the boundaries of Parrotland. He met birds in this unknown land, but none were parrots. The new birds were courteous to the Important Parrot, but did not give him the applause he knew and loved so well in Parrotland. This made him so lonely and depressed he hastened back to Parrotland, where he was once more applauded. But he had caught a glimpse of something he could never forget."

SINCERE MOTIVES

"Since sincere motives must accompany us to these classes, how can we judge ourselves in this?"

"It happens all by itself. Sincere people come back persistently, for they want truth more than wanting ego-gratification. Insincere people depart, usually with harsh criticism."

"Why do they criticize?"

"The false self fears destruction at the hands of truth, so criticism is their handy but useless weapon for striking back."

HUMAN DECEPTION

"After attending these classes I am seeing through human deception much better than formerly. For instance, when wanting something for himself a man will always try to persuade you that it is for your benefit.''

"Yes, the rock of self-interest is hidden by a forest of smooth words.''

"Please say more about deception.''

"You can be deceived by another person only when you want something from him, perhaps money or comfort, sex or flattery. You cannot be deceived by someone from whom you want nothing.''

DRAINED

"I feel drained by certain people.''

"You permit it because you want something from them.''

"But each of us needs the other person.''

"You don't need anyone's neurosis.''

"True.''

NOISY MINDS

"In order to make correction, please show us how we misuse our minds.''

"A husband and wife were stranded in an isolated mountain cabin during heavy snows. To keep their minds off their discomfort they played loud music all day long. Because of this they were unable to hear the sounds of a rescue team trying to locate them. People prefer a noisy mind to a receptive one, then wonder why rescuing messages fail to come!''

INTERESTING OBSERVATION

"I have observed something quite interesting. When telling people about these higher truths they become defensive. They assure me they have their own ways for ending anxiety.''

"Did you notice the anxiety with which they assured you?''

ONE WAY OUT

"My wife and I often have our own two-person study group at home. May we have a subject for tomorrow night?''

"Study the following facts. The greater a man's distance from the truth the stronger his illusory belief that he possesses the truth. Such a man is practically unreachable, for you cannot give him something he believes he already possesses. This accounts for the fanatical zeal of the deluded and the neurotic. Connect this with another fact. Awareness of *not* having the truth is the same as an approach to the truth. So awareness of our actual condition is the one way out."

GRIEF AND REGRET

"Why is there so much grief and regret in human relations?"

"Grief and regret can be explained in a single sentence. Foolish people extend invitations which other foolish people accept."

SUPERIOR WISDOM

"Whether we admit it or not, we feel trapped!"

"Man feels like a prisoner condemned to inhabit a remote and lonely island. He finds a small boat which carries him a short distance out to sea. But he is then sighted and intercepted by a roving prison ship which returns him to the desolate island. His pattern of escape and capture is repeated endlessly over the years. His great chance for escape consists of full knowledge of the island, the sea, and his captors. Man is really more intelligent than his captors, but fails to exercise his superior wisdom."

FAME

"From this higher viewpoint, what is fame?"

"Fame is nothing more than thousands of people thinking about a particular person. This mass-thinking may see him as good or bad, but it has no relationship whatever to his actual condition, whatever it may be. Only his own thinking determines his inner state, which means he must not be deluded by public praise. From the viewpoint of God and Reality, fame is meaningless."

PREDICTING HUMAN BEHAVIOR

"It would be valuable to be able to predict human behavior."

"The behavior of mechanical human beings can be predicted with perfect accuracy. Tell someone the painful truth about himself and he will resent it. Fail to carefully examine your confused ideas and a second troubled day must follow the first. Let two insecure people meet for friendship or romance in an effort to escape insecurity and sooner or later they will quarrel. These unhappy patterns can be broken only by awareness of our mechanicalness, which opens the door to conscious action."

REAL SECURITY

"I feel nervous when people do not behave toward me the way I expect."

"Your real security never depends upon any other person behaving toward you in this way or that way. You may think it does, which means you must learn to think from your free mind. Start today."

"As you once said, we make our own fog, but happily, we can also make our own sunlight."

FREEDOM FROM THE STORM!

"Everyone yearns for freedom from the world's chaos."

"Your physical body is in the world, but your cosmic self can remain detached from it. Think of a ship's light penetrating into an ocean storm. Though in the storm, the light remains unaffected by its fury. See why? Because the light has a different nature than the storm. This is why all the great teachers reject surface changes in favor of a totally new nature. By the way, all this is not just lofty words. You have heard about a fact which can be personally experienced by anyone with enough endurance."

REVIEW THESE ENRICHING PRINCIPLES

1. Insight into human nature keeps you wise and safe.

2. You can learn how to live your own free life.
3. These teachings serve as strong rescuing ropes.
4. See through masks to see people as they really are.
5. Observe how your thoughts produce similar experiences.
6. Look for the real world beneath the artificial world.
7. Develop your own powers for finding the way out.
8. Understand yourself and you will understand others.
9. Never permit other people to drain your energy.
10. You are far more intelligent than your problems.

Chapter 5

THE WAY OUT OF PERSONAL PROBLEMS

THE COINS

"We need to remember the importance of remaining in the center of these princely teachings."

"An illustration will help. Imagine a dozen coins resting on a plate. A few of the coins are at the center of the plate, while others are at the edge. If you shake the plate, which coins will remain on it and which will fall off?"

"Life has many shakes, but I can testify to something. These teachings are increasingly helpful in keeping me from falling off the edge."

SOMETHING HIGHER

"I give up trying to solve my particular problem."

"If you really mean it—great!"

"Why is it great?"

"Because something higher than your usual self can now solve it."

SAFETY

"What worries me is the number and the variety of problems attacking me. I can see where one or two of them might vanish, but others are too stubborn."

"Truth is not bothered by the number or the kind of problems you have. Truth solves one or a thousand difficulties with equal ease."

"That is encouraging to hear."

"When reaching the safety of home it makes no difference whether you were caught out in rain or wind or lightning."

THE PROBLEM OF GLOOM

"Please give us a particular viewpoint of our problem."

"The problem is always our inability and unwillingness to study the problem itself. Take gloom. Do people ever see gloom as a self-defeating state, and do they ever see it as an unnecessary pain? Rarely. Not knowing what to do with gloom, people simply wander around and suffer from it. They need to be told that something can be done about gloom and every other painful feeling. They need to study esoteric science, which blows away the clouds of misunderstanding."

THE BOAT

"How do labels prevent cosmic exploration?"

"Four travelers came to a river they wished to cross. A boat was tied to a tree, ready for their use. However, the boat had no name, which caused an argument among three of the travelers. Each insisted that the boat must be named, also, each demanded the right to supply the name. The fourth man listened quietly as the arguers shouted their preferences, which were Ship of Salvation, Heavenly Guide, and Vessel of Light. The fourth man urged them to simply cross, but they refused, so sighing at their foolishness he took the boat across the river."

FREEDOM FROM THE PAST

"I would like freedom from my terrible past."

"You are now free from it."

"But I don't feel it."

"That is because you are thinking instead of realizing. Thought functioning as memory seems to tie you to the past, but it is an illusory rope. When thinking about the past you think about it *now*. Now is all there is, so right now you are free from the past."

GUILT

"Please explain feelings of guilt."

"All guilt is false. It is cunning egotism, usually masquerading as repentance and humility. A guilty man takes great pride in being *someone*. He will continue to hurt himself and others. Only insight into this can make him a good and innocent man."

AUTHENTIC SELF-CHANGE

"What problems do people have when trying to attain authentic self-change?"

"To really change his life a man must find someone who knows more than he does. Now I will ask you a question."

"Yes?"

"What man will admit that someone else knows more than he does? I don't mean a surface admission, or an admission arising from a desperate crisis. Rather, what man will sacrifice his pretense of knowing the answers in order to really change himself?"

"I see the problem."

PUBLIC BEHAVIOR

"I am tense in public because I don't know how I am supposed to behave."

"There! See! You are *supposed* to behave! Why on earth are you supposed to act in a preplanned manner? You do this because you want something out of the social situation. You want attention or approval or sex, or maybe you want others to think you are a nicer person than you really are. Find yourself. You will then have no confusions about the way you are supposed to act. You will be yourself."

THE FISHERMEN

"It is difficult for me to see how I cause my own misfortune."

"Early one morning some Scottish fishermen sailed their boat into a small harbor on an island. The harbor was located at the base of some tall cliffs. Though somewhat remote the harbor had been used many times before, so the fishermen felt they would soon be safely docked. To their surprise the boat ran aground. During the night the cliffs had come loose to spill tons of earth into the harbor. That illustrates man's misfortunes. Unseen forces work at night, jolting his complacency. So make the unseen seen. Become conscious."

AGITATION

"What can I do about my constant state of agitation?"

"Cease to love it."

"Are you saying I am fond of agitation?"

"Yes, and you fear losing it, for agitation supplies a false feeling of aliveness, a quick thrill. It is cosmic law that you cannot retain anything you cease to love. Cease to cherish agitation and it will depart."

THE BUTTERFLY

"Where am I making a mistake?"

"In your present state you are a butterfly caught in the rain. But you make a mistake. Instead of recovering the intelligence by which you could fly out of the rain you just flutter around hating the rain."

"Is it possible for me to recover my intelligence?"

"Of course it is."

"Then at all costs I will recover it."

SELF-COMMAND

"Why do people fail in their quest for self-command?"

"A man is first told that he lacks self-command. He is then told how to attain it through spiritual and psychological principles. At this point he usually makes an incredible mistake that blocks self-command. He mistakes intellectual knowledge about self-command for the actual experience of self-command. He imagines he possesses what he does not possess, which splits him down the middle of his psychic system. This produces the self-righteous teacher and the alcoholic advisor. Self-command appears only as knowledge of ourselves dissolves all that is not ourselves."

WHIRLPOOL

"Take two men, both having problems. One of them is working on himself and the other is not. What is the difference in the two?"

"Both are caught in a whirlpool, but the working man knows he is caught and is actively trying to get out. The other man is so busy *battling* the whirlpool he has neither the intelligence nor the energy to try to get out. He is vainly trying to prove himself superior to the whirlpool, which can be done only by escaping it."

THE NERVOUS ROLE

"I want to stop playing my dramatic and nervous role, but society insists that I remain onstage."

"The stage is within you, so you can walk off any time you like."

"But the role involves earning a living, buying and selling, relations with people."

"You can be involved in all of these without playing the nervous role."

"How?"

"Start by trying to answer your own question."

SELF-RECOVERY

"What is the point in trying to uplift the world? Everyone is equally miserable. The only difference is in the ways people disguise their anguish."

"Never mind everyone else. Think about your own problem."

"All right. I am doing that right now."

"See? You have already eliminated every problem in the world except your own. Now attend to yourself."

"But it seems selfish to attend to myself alone."

"Imagine a hospital having hundreds of patients. Is it selfish for one of them to get well?"

ONE PROBLEM

"It is a world of weary people."

"When people are tired of life they are really tired of themselves."

"I used to think I had dozens of problems, but now I see that I have only one problem—me."

"That is the dawning of a new self."

"I am convinced that any change that does not change human nature is no change at all."

TREASURE MAP

"I seek but never find."

"While searching through an old trunk a man found a piece of paper which seemed to be a treasure map. With great elation he tried to find the treasure, but every trail led nowhere. He was about to give up when he found several other pieces of marked paper in the trunk. He then realized that the first piece of paper had been only part of the map. Now having the whole map he sought and found the treasure. You need a whole cosmic map, which includes knowledge, daring, persistence, and love for the truth."

RIGHT AND WRONG

"All my life I have tried to live by what is right while rejecting what is wrong. My life remains miserable. Where am I making a mistake?"

"In assuming you know the difference between right and wrong."

ASLEEP

"All the great religious teachers and philosophers say that man dwells in a state of psychic sleep. What does it mean to be asleep?"

"In the last few days were you angry or envious or troubled or nervous?"

"Yes."

"That is what it means to be asleep."

HOW TO AVOID TROUBLE

"May I mention one way I have been helped?"

"Please do."

"Help has often come from an idea dropped into a casual conversation with other members of our class. Someone once commented that an arrogant person humbled by a painful crisis will become arrogant again after the crisis. That single idea has kept me out of trouble with certain people."

REPRESENT YOURSELF!

"Why do I feel so inadequate when facing a crisis?"

"Because you are not really there. A story will help. A busy businessman sent other people to represent him at business conferences. But one representative was too nervous to think clearly, another was lazy, and so on. Their misrepresentations caused the businessman endless grief. Dismissing them, he represented himself on future occasions. Likewise, you must not let acquired habits misrepresent you. Represent yourself. Let your real nature be present. It handles every challenge perfectly."

HURT AND DISAPPOINTMENT

"Why do I get hurt and disappointed so often?"

"Because you never take the unexpected into account. You hope favorable factors will continue as they are. This hope hardens into a fearful demand. But since life is constant change your hopes and demands bump into the unexpected many times daily, causing hurt and disappointment."

"How can I correct this?"

"See that your real nature is never apart from change,

but is really one with it. In this wholeness with life there can be no hurt or disappointment.''

BREAKDOWN

''Please discuss human breakdown.''

.''When offered the choice between a large and shiny car and a smaller and plain car, a wise man examines both cars carefully. People attracted to the shiny car might find it too faulty for daily use. Man selects large and shiny illusions, then wonders why he breaks down. A breakdown can range from a minor irritation to a severe crisis. Breakdown is the puncturing of the pretense that one knows what he is doing with his life. Pursue these studies and you will come to the end of breakdowns.''

EXTERIOR GOODNESS

''In reading three different books recently I noticed how each teacher cautioned against the same mistake. They said we must not believe that exterior acts of goodness always indicate a good nature. Why is this point emphasized so much?''

''Because covering yourself with bird's feathers cannot make you fly.''

COSMIC UNDERSTANDING

''My question is how can I act correctly while in the midst of changing and challenging conditions?''

''Develop cosmic understanding. This understanding is like a master clock in a school or factory. Keeping right time itself it sends electrical messages to dozens of other clocks throughout the building, making each of them as right as itself. Cosmic understanding operates accurately and effortlessly, whether in home or office, whether in a conversation or in a new and unexpected condition.''

STUDY GROUP

''We have a small study group in another city. Please give me an idea to bring back to our next meeting.''

"Stop arguing with an unwanted psychological condition and it will disappear."

"You mean like feeling inferior and rejected?"

"Yes. Such feelings have no power except that which is given them by argument. Have you ever noticed how you mentally argue with an unwanted condition? Drop the argument and you drop the feeling. Try it."

"Our group is tired of arguing. We want to change."

THE BORROWER

"Why am I so uncomfortable?"

"Because you are a psychological borrower."

"What does that mean?"

"It means you are wearing another man's coat—a coat that does not fit you."

PROBLEMS WITH PEOPLE

"May we have a fundamental fact about the problems human beings have with each other?"

"You have no problem until you make one. The problem is built out of the mechanical movements of your own mind. In its insecurity the mind tries to make itself secure by demanding that others behave according to personal desire. But this breeds even more insecurity. This fact is beyond the perception of most people, which is why they remain afraid. With energetic inquiry, you can be different."

A POPULAR ILLUSION

"Help us see through a popular but damaging illusion."

"Take the illusion of self-control. Imagine yourself standing on shore while watching a boat battle its way through a storm. You admire the way the boat zigzags through the waves as it moves toward the harbor. Later, you congratulate the captain for his skilled performance, but his reply is a surprise. He informs you he was out of control all the time, for the boat had lost its rudder. Likewise, man only appears to have self-command. Just watch his so-called control when his desires are frustrated. Control comes with self-knowledge.''

DESCRIPTION

''Describe to me the nature of this new life.''

''Describe to me the taste of a peach.''

RESENTMENT

''Please discuss resentment.''

''In one sense resentment is always self-resentment. Take someone entering a social situation. Reminding himself of the role he must play for social acceptance he laughs at the jokes or expresses serious concern when told about someone's misfortune. His forced behavior is in sharp conflict with his natural self, which he painfully feels. Out of this comes resentment of his own weakness, which he can neither understand nor cure.''

''You have just described me. I am tired of living up to what others expect of me. This information can start the cure.''

HANDLING DAILY EVENTS

''How can we meet daily events correctly?''

''Everything that happens to you proves a cosmic law of one kind or another. Learn all about that law instead of resisting or resenting it.''

''People want a way that will never go wrong.''

''Place cosmic knowledge first and you will never go wrong.''

OBSTACLE

''I wish to find the way out, and feel I have made at least preliminary progress. Since you have studied me over the months, perhaps you know where I am still standing in my own way. So please, what is my chief obstacle to finding the answers?''

''The unconscious assumption that you already know the answers.''

MISUNDERSTANDING

"We have accumulated so many uncomfortable habits."

"Yes, through misunderstanding. It is like the story of the boy and his socks. On Monday the boy's mother told him to put on clean socks every morning. By Thursday he couldn't get his shoes on."

THE WHOLE PROBLEM

"We are unconscious that we are unconscious. That is the whole problem."

"Correct. So anything experienced consciously can never be a problem, for problems exist only in unconscious action. You have difficulty walking around your home only when the lights are out."

RIGHT ASSOCIATION

"People drain and exhaust me."

"Never without your permission."

"But I don't give permission."

"Association is permission."

"But I feel lonely."

"Only because you do not have right self-association."

HOW TO STOP RUNNING

"Thanks to these teachings I am beginning to see that what I have called happiness is not happiness at all. That is a new start toward the real product."

"Artificial happiness can be illustrated. It is like a man who runs from one hilltop to another and shouts out to people below. Getting excited at being the object of attention he calls it happiness. He never notices the long periods of dejection he suffers from while running between hilltops. This system shows you how to be happy without wearily running anywhere."

"That is what I want—to stop running."

IDENTITY

"Who am I?"

"Discover who you are not."

"Who am I not?"

"You are neither your self-descriptions nor the descriptions given you by others."

"But who am I?"

"Someone who needs no descriptions."

HOW THE WORLD WORKS

"I am giving special attention to a recent lesson in class by trying to see through self-deception. Please suggest a specific area for investigation."

"In his incredible vanity man assumes he knows how this world works. No matter how often his spills and heartaches tell him different, he never sees through the deceptive game he plays on himself. For example, someone deludes himself into thinking that personal advantages bring security. He never sees his haunting fear of losing his so-called advantages. He could learn how the world works if only he would stop pretending he already knows."

THE PROBLEM OF FAILURE

"How can I solve the problem of personal failure?"

"By seeing that the problem itself is false."

"I do not understand."

"There is no personal failure or success because there is no personal self to create either one. The *idea* of a personal self creates the *idea* of personal failure or success. You must see the falsity of the problem itself, and when the light flashes, what a moment!"

HELPFUL THOUGHT

"I would like to mention a thought that has been of great help in a problem I have had with some friends."

"Yes, please go ahead."

"You said that knowledge of human nature makes us strong in human relations. This idea first made me aware of how weak I was when with others. It then energized my intention to understand human nature in order to command myself when with others."

ELIMINATE WRONG IDEAS

"I want to find the way out, but everything is so vague."

"Suppose you want to locate a certain recipe in a cookbook. You know it is somewhere in the book, but do not know the right page. So you go through the book to eliminate all the wrong pages until finding the right one. Likewise, the way out exists within you. Have no doubt about that. Perform the intelligent task of eliminating wrong ideas, after which the way out *must* appear."

FEELINGS OF REJECTION

"Psychologically, what happens when I feel rejected?"

"What happens when you toss a rubber ball against a wall? It bounces back. You toss out your expectations of how other people should treat you, then get hurt when they refuse to accept you at your own value. The real cause of your rejection was your expectation. Most people fear to live without expecting agreement from others, but you must not be like most people. If you want feelings of rejection to stop bouncing back at you, dare to live with no expectations at all."

FOR YOURSELF

"I find it difficult to please someone I want to please in order to hold him."

"You are the slave of anyone you want to please for that reason. You cannot please anyone who needs you to please him; you can only temporarily suspend his displeasure. Try living your own life. If that does not please him he must solve his own problem. This is not selfishness or disloyalty. It is something you must do for yourself."

MAGIC TRICKS

"In seeking the way out, what must we guard against?"

"One day a traveling charlatan visited a village to sell his cheap products. To attract a crowd and to win its approval he stood on a box and performed several magic tricks. The magic tricks so dulled the minds of the villagers that they eagerly bought the worthless products. The next day another traveler arrived, one with products of high quality. In simple language he explained the value of his goods. But because he performed no magic tricks, no one paid attention."

REAL MAGIC

"I am in great despair."

"Yes, and you unwisely waste it."

"Pardon?"

"Like most people, you foolishly waste your despair. Come to this class with a humble spirit—and I don't mean a faked humble spirit—and I will teach you psychic magic. You will learn how to use despair."

"For what purpose?"

"To end despair."

"That is real magic!"

TALKING

"Sometimes I talk foolishly and impulsively, which I later regret."

"A man who talks from himself—from his original nature—never talks himself into trouble."

UNIVERSAL WORLD

"We lead such limited lives. Why?"

"An unaware man knows no other world than the self-centered world built with his thoughts and beliefs. He insists that this world is the only one with a right to exist, which breeds violence. In public he may appear to welcome the equally illusory worlds of other people, but it is just another part of his stage performance. With self-interest foremost he simply uses other people as allies. Together they keep the mass delusion alive, and usually end up fighting each other. We must burst through the limited world of conditioned thought to enter the unlimited Universal World.''

THE FOXES

''By what process do we free ourselves from false teachings?''

''Through cosmic maturity. A large and crafty fox told a falsehood to a young and innocent fox. For selfish reasons the large fox told the young fox that salty sea water was healthier than water from the forest stream. The taste of the young fox told him a different story, but he was too dominated by the older fox to do more than suspect the cruel hoax. But in time the small fox became a large and independent fox who realized that the forest water alone was healthy.''

WHAT YOU WILL SEE

''At the last class you said we would sooner or later see things quite clearly. What are some of them?''

''You will see that every problem is caused by forgetting your real nature. You will see that trying to conform to frantic society is like trying to dance in rhythm with an erupting volcano. You will see that the only worthwhile life is one which seeks to understand what life is really all about.''

PERSONAL AFFAIRS

''I never know how much of my private life I should reveal to others. Some people almost demand to know about my personal affairs.''

''The truth alone has the right to know about your private life, and you must permit it to do so. That alone makes your personal affairs what you want them to be.''

NEW HOME

"My greatest fear is that I will be unable to repair my present nature."

"Don't try to repair it. Get a new nature. A man once lived fearfully in a home with walls having many dangerous cracks. Not knowing what else to do he covered the cracks with pretty pictures. He fooled a few people, but since his own mind was not deceived he suffered great anguish. His suffering ended when he learned how to build a completely new and different home."

VITAL INFORMATION ABOUT THE WAY OUT

1. Remain in the center of these wealthy teachings.
2. Truth solves all human problems with equal ease.
3. The past casts no shadows on a man with cosmic light.
4. Your real nature is in full harmony with change.
5. The end of illusion is the end of painful breakdown.
6. One of your aims is to have right self-association.
7. This system teaches us how to stop running wearily.
8. A problem vanishes with awareness of its false power.
9. It is real magic to use despair to end despair.
10. You can build a new nature which has no problems.

Chapter 6

HOW TO WIN TRUE POWER AND COURAGE

THE DELICIOUS MELON

"How can we pass beyond the words to the experience?"

"A band of travelers in ancient Persia were invited to spend the night at the mansion of a wealthy merchant. At dinner the guests were served a delicious melon. So superior was the melon's taste that every guest except one praised the merchant for it. The silent guest was silent because he was busy placing the melon's seeds into his pocket. Observing this, the merchant nodded in approval, for he knew that the silent guest was also wise."

REAL CONFIDENCE

"I am willing to do whatever is necessary to attain real confidence."

"Real confidence comes into view by understanding the nature of artificial confidence. False confidence must have the support of as many people as it can get, which means that mobs and crowds have artificial confidence. False confidence hopes that the future will be better than the present, but the person with this artificiality fails to realize that his present nature must repeat itself in the future. Only a man's real self has real confidence, which is natural and effortless."

FALSE POWER

"I am afraid of a certain condition which has dreadful power over me."

"Your fear of it *is* its power over you, and its *only* power. No condition has power over you unless you give it power by fearing it. When fully realizing this you will feel able to move mountains."

DIFFERENT KIND OF EXCITEMENT

"I would just like to say that these studies get more exciting as I go along. The excitement is hard to explain, but I know that you know what I mean."

"It is a different kind of excitement, isn't it?"

"Yes, unlike anything I had ever known before. Its refreshment endures throughout the day, regardless of what happens to me in the exterior world. I have finally found what I have been seeking all my life."

SEA BIRD

"I would appreciate an explanation of a recent point. You stated that psychological comfort prevents us from rising into understanding."

"A man gains a certain comfortable feeling by clinging to fixed ideas. But it is false comfort, for he must nervously defend his ideas against everyone with opposing ideas. So his so-called comfort prevents him from rising above mere ideas to total understanding. Do you know why nature gives sea birds longer and stronger wings than land birds? Because sea birds fly vast stretches of ocean without coming down to land. Be a sea bird. Soar."

RIDING

"I study hard but go nowhere."

"The ability to describe the characteristics of a horse is not the same as riding it up the mountain."

"What prevents me from riding?"

"Your fear that the horse may head in a direction you don't want to go."

"But what if he does just that?"

"Ride in fear if necessary, but have the courage to ride on."

ORIGINAL NATURE

"You say we must recover our original nature. What is meant?"

"Imagine yourself leaving the light to enter a dark tunnel. When exiting from the tunnel you recover the light you used to enjoy. Come out into your original nature."

ENCOURAGEMENT

"Please explain the role played by encouragement."

"Right encouragement is a confirmation that you are heading in the right direction. Very beneficial, it can come only from someone who has found the way out for himself. A correct idea from a teacher is picked up by a similar though weaker idea in the student. The confirmation of the student's own correct idea encourages and strengthens him. Suppose a small girl wants a certain kind of bead from a sewing basket. Selecting a bead she asks her older sister whether it is the right bead. The older girl's affirmation encourages the judgment of the younger girl."

USE IT!

"How am I responsible for my own feelings?"

"Why were you disappointed yesterday?"

"Because a friend failed to act the way I desired."

"It was your thought about his action that caused the disappointment. It is your wrong thought about *anything* that causes disappointment or any other negative feeling. You are always responsible for your own feelings, which is not a fearful fact, but a great opportunity. Use it!"

INQUIRE WITHIN

"We are too timid for our own good!"

"Yes, so great audacity is required. It is like a man in a dizzy spell standing out in the nighttime cold while looking through a window into a warm and comfortable home. He wonders whether he will be welcomed inside by whoever lives there. In his dizziness he is unaware that *he* lives there. He must daringly inquire within.''

HOW SELF-INSIGHT ADVANCES

''Tell us something about the process of self-enlightenment.''

''Happily, one insight leads to the next. See how uncomfortable you are with people and you see how you have unnecessarily made yourself their slave. See the need to stop pretending and you see how to end the fear of being found out. See how a wrong thought precedes a wrong action and you see how to stay out of wrong places.''

''We need more of that kind of internal vigilence.''

FOOTPRINTS

''I try to follow the footprints of men like Christ, but stumble.''

''Don't follow anyone's footprints. That is imitation, not devotion. Nature never duplicates a path. Listen to the wisdom of men like Christ, then make your own footprints. That is precisely what every authentic teacher urges.''

SELF-FINDING

''How can I find myself?''

''Every lost person is lost because he foolishly insists upon playing it safe.''

''What does that mean?''

''It means you prefer anger and resistance when truth tries to tell you how to find yourself. Anger is a foolish attempt to play it safe by defending the very ideas which cause misery. It is like a man who tries to escape captivity by hiding in a prison. Can you think of anything more ridiculous?''

ROPE

''When will we be able to grasp the rescuing rope of an awakened man?''

''When the rope he offers is the same rope you want.''

AUTHENTIC INDIVIDUALITY

"Help us to think rightly about authentic individuality."

"Some travelers hiking across the countryside agreed to help each other carry the needed supplies. But the agreement was not as noble as it appeared. Each man cunningly tried to overload another, while carrying as little as possible himself. So they journeyed forward with brooding hostility, which often erupted into physical violence. One day, when reaching a fork in the path, one man announced his intention of leaving the group to make his own trail. He said he would carry his own supplies and would never again permit anyone to falsely burden him. That individual reached a different destination than the others."

LOYALTY

"I was called disloyal when I declined to follow a set of traditional beliefs offered to me."

"It is not disloyal to think with your own mind. The only real loyalty consists of being true to your own nature."

NEW SONG

"Why do people find life so dull and repetitious?"

"Because most people are like a singer who has learned only one song. No matter what he is requested to sing he always comes out with the same song, usually an unhappy one. Even when it is to his own benefit to sing another melody he cannot do so. So he bores himself and everyone around him. Do you know people like that?"

"Yes, and I must face the same thing in myself. That is why I like being part of this group. I am learning a new song."

DOUBT

"I am whirled around by uncertainty and doubt."

"Think carefully toward what I am about to tell you.

You can be doubtful only when you do not really know
what you imagine you know. Therefore, can you face the
fact that you really do not know something about yourself
or about life?''

"Yes. Self-facing is now an absolute necessity."

"Good. That will be the beginning of true knowledge
and the ending of all doubt."

NEGATIVITY

"The other day I was discussing these principles with a
friend. He insisted that it is a negative practice to observe
and admit how confused we are. He claimed we should
think only about bright topics."

"It is not negative to see a negative fact about yourself. It is negative to fearfully refuse to face the negativity."

FOX AND SHEEP

"One thing seems endless—human gullibility."

"An animal kingdom was once ruled by an evil fox.
One day the sheep in his kingdom felt unhappy with their
miserable conditions, and threatened to revolt. The fox
hastily called for advice from his chief minister, a cunning
crow. The fox asked how he could keep the sheep in a
dazed submission. Smiling, the crow assured the fox that
it was very simple. All he had to do was to continue to
treat the sheep like sheep while *calling* them lions."

DECEPTIVE TEACHINGS

"Up to this point in my life it seems likely that I have
been accepting solutions which solve nothing."

"Perhaps sometime you tried to erase pencil writing in
an attempt to correct a mistake, only to find that the un-
clean eraser only made the original problem worse. That
is what happens when we carelessly accept false solutions
and deceptive teachings. A deceptive teaching is one which
does not agree with your own real nature."

HOW TO REMAIN UNTOUCHED

"At one time you asked us to mention ideas which struck us with special impact. I will tell you about one such idea. In one lecture you said that we can remain untouched by future events which become disasters to other people. You said that this victory is achieved through diligent inner preparation."

"Right. Noah wisely built the ark before it rained."

MENTAL FOG

"I admit I am in a mental fog."

"What are you in a fog about?"

"It's too foggy to tell."

"Very good. Only those who know they do not know can find the way out."

FLIGHT

"A part of me claims that I will never get off the ground."

"Pay no attention to that part. Start with whatever you can do, and soon you will do what you formerly thought was impossible. Some birds lived on an isolated island. Though having wings they did not understand their use. One day they were visited by birds from another island who urged the isolated birds to use their wings for flight. The grounded birds refused at first, for they believed their wings were merely strange weights. But they listened, learned, and flew."

THINK CAREFULLY

"The only way most people change is in the ways they pretend to change. I seek something truly different. I want authentic self-transformation."

"How badly do you want it? Enough to abandon the familiar? It is very simple. If you want something different you cannot cling to the familiar. It is one or the other. You cling to the familiar without knowing you do, which is why awareness of yourself is essential.''

''I will think carefully about all this.''

CHERRY BLOSSOMS

''I feel the importance of having right intentions in this class.''

''Just as cherry blossoms promise forthcoming fruit, so do sincere intentions promise future self-newness.''

EXPLANATIONS

''I need explanations.''

''Life explains itself to everyone who asks.''

''What should I ask?''

''Ask what prevents self-transformation.''

''What prevents self-transformation?''

''A combination of an inability and a refusal to listen to anything outside of yourself. Both ability and receptivity can be developed, but first you must realize and admit your present inability and refusal to listen.''

STARTLING REALIZATION

''At the start of my studies I learned something that helped enormously. I learned that we can go nowhere while still clinging to our fixed thinking habits.''

''What made you aware of the need to think in a totally new way?''

''The startling realization that I was not really going anywhere. It was shocking but enlightening. Do you know how far I traveled with my hardened mind? About as far as you can throw a stove!''

A PERSONAL EXPERIENCE

''From personal experience I know the truth of something we talked about recently. The class discussed the idea that no one can be attracted to cosmic facts until he is ready for them. But I also know the reverse of that. Once a man has run out of phony excuses, nothing can keep him away.''

"True. A man must reach the point where he can no longer go along with self-deception. Then, nothing can keep him away. The ancient philosopher Antisthenes was such a man. Every day he hiked five miles into Athens, just to learn from Socrates.''

BORROWED MAP

"As a practical project you instructed us to observe ourselves in daily action. What revelations! Yesterday I noticed how nervous I am when not acting from my natural self.''

"Yes, it's the kind of insecurity you feel when studying a borrowed map. Its knowledge can be taken away at any moment. These teachings show you how to own your own map.''

HAVE AN INNER EXPERIENCE

"Nothing new ever happens to me. Everything is old and boring.''

"A new experience must occur inwardly. It happens when you don't know what to do about something and then courageously remain with that not-knowing. This interrupts habitual thought and makes room for a liberating experience. For example, there are few pleasures as delicious—and as self-destructive—as the thrill of catching another person in a mistake or in a disgrace. You must refuse that known pleasure, that mechanical reaction, for new experiences are far above their level.''

CAREER

"Can these teachings help my career?''
"Of course.''
"How?''
"By preventing you from being a slave to it.''

ARTIFICIAL NEEDS

"If we learn how to stay out of the swamp in the first place, we will not have to struggle to get out. That is the knowledge I want."

"What are you doing to acquire this knowledge?"

"I am trying to identify and abolish artificial needs, such as the need to outwit other people and have advantages over them."

ICEBREAKERS

"No doubt it is wrong to become dependent upon a teacher. How can this error be avoided?"

"An authentic teacher makes self-reliance a part of his program. A man who really knows is like one of those powerful ships that patrol icy seas. Having immense strength in its prow, the ship breaks through an ice field, making a trail of open water for other ships to follow. But there is something else. A man of real knowledge does not aim to make followers out of listeners. He shows them how to become icebreakers themselves."

SUPREME FACT!

"I don't know what to do with my life."

"Because you wander away from a supreme fact of life."

"What fact?"

"The fact that life is the way you see it. You now see life as chaotic because you are your own world of chaos. But there is an inspiring way to see life."

"How does this help me know what to do with my life?"

"When inspired you have nothing to do but live lightly."

EXCEPTION

"You know, when first hearing that people work against their true interests I used to think that I was the exception to the rule."

"Any person can be the exception to the rule, but must first realize that he is not."

COSTLY THRILLS

"You are able to tell us why we behave as we do, so please explain something. Yesterday I accused someone of doing something wrong, then was ashamed when discovering he was innocent. Why was I so eager to accuse him?"

"Because you acted with a mechanical desire to get an emotional thrill from the incident. That is the only behavior pattern of which you are presently capable."

"How can mechanicalness be replaced with conscious behavior?"

"Be aware of your desire for a thrill and then have the sense to drop it. Thrills cost more than you can afford. Above the thrill of accusing another is self-command."

DEFINITE CHANGE

"Several of us discussed a point from yesterday's class. You spoke of a definite change that eventually takes place after diligent investigation. Could you illustrate this certain change?"

"It is like a hiker standing on a low hill in the desert, while sighting a town in the distance. While realizing you have not as yet arrived, you know the right direction to take."

WHAT MAN FEARS

"What do I fear?"

"You fear yourself."

"I never thought of it like that. Please expand the idea."

"You fear your wild impulsiveness, fear that others will see through you, fear your inability to behave correctly."

"All that is true. And I can change?"

"Yes, by becoming a quiet but alert listener."

"I realize that learning must precede changing."

SELF-RELIANCE

"I am convinced of the need for developing the basic virtues, such as self-reliance."

"Self-reliance exists on two levels. On the everyday level, self-reliance is developed by acquiring knowledge. You can then rely on yourself for building a house or repairing a car. But a higher form of self-reliance is needed for uplifting the inner person. This superior self-reliance consists of no longer accepting all the wrong descriptions of ourselves collected over the years. This produces uncertainty at first, but this very not-knowing-who-we-are leads to real knowing."

RETURN TO SIMPLICITY

"If only we could return to inner simplicity!"

"There is so little simplicity in this world its rare appearance can hardly be recognized. People in the habit of clawing their way through the jungle take a clear section as something unnatural and undesirable. There is only one way to start the return to simplicity, which is to clearly see your punishment at the hands of complexity."

HOW TO END SELF-LIMITATION

"I feel limited in everything I do."

"Sit down at a table with paper and pencil. Close your eyes and write two sentences. See how limited and how awkward you feel? Open your eyes and look at your writing. You could have done much better had you not limited yourself. People feel limited in life because of self-imposed psychic limitations. In yesterday's class you were told to open your spiritual eyes. You can begin to open them by deeply desiring to end self-limitation."

COSMIC COURAGE

"During our last meeting you spoke of cosmic courage. What is an example of this?"

"It is cosmic courage to continue to study these principles when they are puzzling and when they do not agree with what you already believe."

EXAMINATION

"What would you advise for someone who cannot as yet sense the value of these teachings?"

"Close examination."

"As someone here remarked, you can't catch the perfume of a rose until coming close."

ENTER THE ROOM

"I feel like someone standing at the door of a dark room. I know I must enter, but am apprehensive."

"The dark room you fear exists within yourself and nowhere else. See how this simplifies everything? The room is at hand, you can enter at once. You need not chase around in vain any more. I will show you what to do. Bravely step into the dark room without having a light in your hand. Now stay there, no matter how nervous you are. Stay there long enough and the light will come on of itself. The light is your new understanding."

POWER

"Please explain the idea of power."

"A man wishing no power according to human definition possesses total power in the spiritual definition."

SPIRITUAL SAYINGS

"I would like to know more about certain spiritual sayings. We are told that whoever abandons his life will find it. Also, to live without security is to have security. There appears to be contradiction in each of these, but I know there is not."

"Abandon artificial life and you find real life. Live without man-made ideas about security and you find ease within the Cosmic Whole."

THE WAY

"How can I find the way?"

"Really want it."

"That is all?"

"Remember, I said to really want it."

INTENTIONS

"I would like to study with right intentions."

"Two men entered a library filled with books of true knowledge. The first man stayed all day long and came out the same man who had entered. The second man stayed ten minutes and came out with a refreshed mind. The first man read in order to impress others with his knowledge. The second man read to learn."

PROFITABLE TALK

"I would like to sit down with you for some profitable talk."

"Everything depends upon your definition of profitable talk."

"I would like to talk about ways to prevent someone from leaving me."

"It would be far more profitable to discuss why you are a slave to that person."

THE OBSERVER

"I know I am my own problem, but it seems that nothing can set me free from myself."

"I want you to remember one thing. You have an inner observer which can calmly stand aside from life's conflicts instead of being involved in them. Please repeat that in your own words."

"I can stand outside myself and simply watch what happens, like a neutral referee at a football game."

"Set yourself free by remembering and practicing that."

HOW WAVERING ENDS

"I waver in the face of life."

"Only one thing prevents wavering, which is to live within the Truth which never wavers. But you must actually live within it, not just imagine you do."

"Living in self-pleasing imagination is probably my problem."

"So you see the necessity for going deeply into these matters?"

"Yes, I definitely see that. Up to this point in my life I have been about as deep as a bowl of soup!"

PATIENCE

"Tell us about something we need for the self-adventure."

"In Peru there is a rocky cliff which at first glance reveals nothing unusual. But wait patiently until the afternoon sun strikes the cliff in a certain way. You will then see the perfect outline of a five-pointed star. In self-adventuring, have more patience while letting the unseen reveal itself."

GOLD MINE

"What idea might encourage a bewildered beginner?"

"At first our inner task is like a gold mine which must be worked for awhile before gold is brought to the surface, but it is still right work."

"Please suggest a profitable way of thinking."

"Too many people have butterfly thoughts, having no aim and no reward. Be wiser. Reflect upon a single theme until thought turns into light."

SUPPORT

"What is the difference between artificiality and Reality?"

"You must wearily support artificiality, while Reality supports you."

BE ON YOUR OWN SIDE!

"One of my first realizations in this class was that I was not on my own side. For instance I saw that harsh judgment toward others was nothing but a self-righteous sense of superiority. I now see how this feeling works against me, not for me."

"Do you see how being on your own side is the same thing as self-unity?"

"Yes, and I see something else. The grasping of these facts is all that really matters."

PSYCHIC ENERGIES

"I seem to lack energy for the inner adventure."

"Picture the underground water system of a town. Water pipes travel in different directions. Some provide drinking water, others serve a factory, some keep the town's trees green. Man's energies are like that. They have full power to serve every human need, but man lacks practical knowledge about them. Some energies are used wrongly, as when annoyance takes the place of understanding. Other energies do not have enough pressure to do their work, as when we fail to go all out for the inner adventure."

STRENGTHENING IDEAS FROM CHAPTER 6

1. Pass beyond the words to the personal experience.
2. Your real self possesses easy and total confidence.
3. Eagerly grasp the rescuing rope offered by reality.
4. Exercise the cosmic wings you definitely possess.
5. Let these facts abolish all fear of yourself.
6. Show cosmic courage by persisting when puzzled.
7. Power over yourself is the only power you need.
8. Have patience toward yourself during the climb.
9. Place yourself and keep yourself on your own side.
10. Wisely use psychic energies for self-advancement.

Chapter 7

YOUR COSMIC MIND KNOWS THE WAY OUT

FOG

"I worry constantly. What is the cause and cure?"

"Worry is simply a lack of consciousness and understanding. It exists only on a lower level of the mind. A passenger worriedly paced the deck of a ship caught in a fog. As the captain approached the passenger voiced his fear of a collision with another ship. Nodding in understanding, the captain invited the passenger to accompany him to the bridge. Doing so, the passenger found himself above the fog's level, where vision was clear. Raise your level of understanding. Where is the fog and where is the worry? Nowhere."

MIND AND BODY

"Please illustrate the connection between mind and body."

"Have you ever noticed how the body obeys the thought? Think of food and the body heads for the refrigerator. Think of entertainment and the legs move toward the television set. With enough watchfulness you can see how thoughts do indeed place the physical body wherever it finds itself, for either benefit or harm. This insight arouses powerful motivation for thinking only constructive thoughts."

LOGIC AND ILLOGIC

"Why does plain logic fail to penetrate a person suffering from self-defeating actions?"

"You cannot talk logic to a man whose illogic pays him either financial or vanity-building benefits."

"That is perfect logic."

WRONG THINKING

"I don't want people to be disappointed with me."

"Give up that kind of thinking."

"But why is it wrong to hope to please people?"

"Because it is nervous slavery."

"I never thought of it like that."

"Think of it like that from now on."

WHY IT HAPPENS

"Why do events happen to us as they do?"

"They happen because of your psychological location, that is, your high or low level of consciousness. Imagine a man dwelling in the desert. Wherever he walks he finds that sand gets into his clothes. He wisely realizes that the reason for this is his geographical location. If he wants to get rid of the uncomfortable sand he must move out of the desert. Anyone wanting different events, higher events, must move out of his psychological desert."

EVERYTHING!

"Everything depends upon how a certain circumstance turns out."

"Everything depends upon the way your mind works."

HOW TO BE UNAFRAID

"Help us to not be afraid."

"You are afraid only because you react to daily life with the memories of former fears. The pure present moment has no fear in it."

"So our task is to see how mere memories rush in to ruin the liberty in the present moment?"

"Yes. This requires constant watchfulness of your responses. You will then learn how to stand free in the fearless present moment, which does not reside in time, and which is free of past and future."

THOUGHT AND FEELING

"Today I made one of those interesting discoveries you said we would make. I noticed how right thought creates calm feeling."

"When the wind stops blowing, the lake stops rippling."

THE PICTURE

"How do we misuse imagination?"

"A prisoner of war was confined in a cell having a single window. He tried to forget his pain by covering the window's bars with a self-made drawing. The drawing showed him in a great auditorium, surrounded by admiring men and attractive women. When feeling depressed he looked at the picture and imagined it as being his real life. But covering the bars with the pretty picture really did nothing for him; he knew it was all a fake. That is how psychic prisoners misuse imagination. The picture must come down. The bars must be faced. Then, intelligent plans for escape can begin."

NEW KIND OF MIND

"Can we say that our aim is to develop a totally new kind of mind?"

"Yes. Otherwise we must suffer from the old mind which torments itself with its own ignorance, like a bird attacking its reflection in a mirror."

"What a relief to know that there is a way out!"

HOW TO MAKE LIFE EASY

"I know my life would be easy if I could just discover how it really works."

"There is a way to find out, but it requires much honesty and diligence on your part. To discover how life really works you must first discover how it does *not* work. So think for yourself. Give us an example of how life does *not* work."

"I cannot have my own way and then expect others to pay for the unhappy consequences of having my own way."

"Excellent. Continue to think along those lines."

REAL INTELLIGENCE

"I am now aware that intelligence does not consist of a mere collection of facts, but exactly what is real intelligence?"

"It is a freely flowing whole mind. Our task is to remove the needless barriers to this natural flow. Any negative thought is a barrier, including antagonism, jealousy, self-glorification. An intelligent mind flows freely and quietly, like a mountain brook."

THE PALACE

"Please help us understand the mind."

"A king of ancient Persia built a magnificent palace on top of a mountain. The lower levels, including the kitchen, dining hall and living quarters, served the everyday needs of the residents. At the very top of the palace was a single room with wide windows on all sides which provided a spectacular view of skies and stars. The mind works in a similar manner. Though a single mind, it works in various ways. The part we call memory serves our everyday needs, while a higher part enables us to see the whole world without personal reference. We must learn to use each part correctly."

SILENT SPACE

"I am overwhelmed by floods of thoughts."

"There is a silent space between two thoughts. Find it and remain there for awhile."

"But without thought I won't know who I am. There will be a nothingness."

"Exactly."

"But this is terrifying."

"Not at all. It is fulfillment at last."

WISDOM FOR TODAY

"Give us wisdom for today."

"Live as if every thought, good or bad, open or secret, comes back to you. It does."

ORIGINAL INTELLIGENCE

"I have lots of answers, but they do nothing for me."

"That is like saying you have a good memory but forget to use it. If you really have the answers they are definite energies which gradually bring your life under your own control."

"I don't understand."

"Your original intelligence understands. Why don't you make the necessary effort to reunite yourself with it?"

"Fair enough."

HARMFUL ILLUSION

"Since the uncovering of illusions is a major aim of ours, please discuss one of them."

"Suppose a man's television set breaks down. Knowing that he knows nothing about repair he either teaches himself or finds an expert repairman. But does he proceed as intelligently when *he* breaks down? Rarely. Without understanding even his smallest moods and motives he deceives himself into thinking he knows just how to make things right. The fact that his repair-work never really repairs anything never occurs to him. So remember, one of man's most harmful illusions is the illusion that he already understands himself."

IDEA

"I want to change my life, but everything seems against it."

"The idea of everything being against self-change is *only* an idea. Get rid of the idea and then see whether anything is against self-change."

WHAT CANNOT HAPPEN

"I am beginning to see what can happen, for instance, things happen for our true benefit once we realize the nature of a true benefit."

"Good, but to see the whole picture you must also understand what cannot happen."

"What cannot happen?"

"Nothing good can happen to an individual until he realizes his extreme suggestibility. Beneficial instruction cannot happen to anyone who fails to distinguish between beneficial and useless instruction."

COSMIC CONSCIOUSNESS

"What the world needs is clear and impersonal judgment."

"Of course, but where will you find it? When a man divides the world into good people and bad people you can be quite sure of how he classifies himself. Clear and impersonal judgment exists only in the individual who has attained cosmic consciousness."

COMPLETE COMMAND

"Peace of mind is such an elusive prize."

"There is only one way to be totally at ease in every condition of life. I will repeat that in different words. There is a certain state of mind which gives you complete command of everything that happens to you."

"You make us eager to know what it is."

"It is a state of mind in which you never need to prove you are right."

HIGH MEADOW

"The battle against circumstances is so endless."

"The battle *against* circumstances can never be won, however, you can place yourself above them with these teachings. Picture a man hiking his way along a valley

trail overgrown with weeds and bushes. He would be foolish to stop and fight every bush. Wisdom tells him to
swiftly hike up the trail until reaching the higher level of
the flowered meadow.''

HOW TO END CONFUSION

''What should I do about my mental confusion?''

''Neither fear nor avoid confusion. People try to avoid
confusion by clinging to adopted attitudes and positions.
They do this in a frantic effort to feel secure, to feel right.
But not only does it perpetuate confusion but it arouses all
sorts of weird and harmful actions. Since their rightness is
illusory, such people easily crack up. Confusion is ended by
voluntarily dropping conditioned ideas about life. You then
live within a Reality which is perfectly clear and competent.''

IMPORTANT THOUGHTS

''The way I occupy my mind determines what happens
to me. That is clear. But it is difficult to know how to occupy the mind profitably.''

''Some things are necessary for the mind to think about,
while other things are both necessary and important. Food
and clothing are necessary topics for the mind, but thoughts
about your life here on earth are both necessary and important. Occupy your mind with important thoughts at
every opportunity.''

THE HOAX

''What is the purpose of self-investigation?''

''Some fleeing robbers put on the uniforms of a ship's
crew and cunningly took over a departing ship. The in-
competent and even hazardous handling of the ship made
the passengers suspicious. Finally seeing through the hoax,
the passengers ordered the robbers to return to port. Man
is taken over by hazardous ideas masquerading as ability.
He must uncover the hoax by investigating his own mind.''

''That is what I call a practical plan.''

UNHAPPY THOUGHT

"How can I fight an unhappy thought?"

"Don't fight. Drop it at once."

"How can I drop it?"

"By dropping it."

INTELLECTUALISM

"I have no confidence in myself."

"Truth has complete confidence in you. You need nothing else."

"But perhaps I have not had enough education."

"Thank heaven. You can approach directly, without the interference of egotistical intellectualism which always pretends it already knows the answers."

HOW TO THINK FOR YOURSELF

"How can I think with my own mind, I mean *really* do so?"

"To begin to think for yourself requires a certain act of courage. You must endure the emptiness of not thinking from your usual ideas and opinions. Make an experiment. The next time you are about to voice an opinion, stop abruptly. You will feel a small discomfort which you will want to relieve by going ahead with your opinion. But do not ease the tension. Stick with it. At this point you will feel something never felt before, which is the awakening of your real mind. It is like the feeling you have when first touching an object lost in the dark."

CRISIS

"How can I handle a forthcoming crisis?"

"If there is no crisis in your mind there is no crisis."

"All of us sense that when the mind is right, so is everything else."

BREAD

"I grasp a few ideas, but the whole meaning escapes me."

"Name an ingredient of bread."

"Flour."

"Name another."

"Salt."

"Name another."

"Water."

"When properly combined, what is the whole and final product?"

"Bread."

"Combine these ideas and the whole meaning takes form."

POINT FOR PONDERING

"Give us a point for pondering until the next meeting."

"The alternation between sunshine and shadow is the alternation of your own mind."

DELUSION

"Exactly what is a delusion?"

"It is a mental mix-up which sees everything backward. What appears good to the deluded man is seen as bad by the awakened man. What seems bad to the sleeping man is seen as good by the enlightened person."

"Details, please."

"The ordinary man loves flattery, which is injurious because it separates him from his real nature. The harmful results of flattery are known only to the awakened man who has freed himself of it."

HOW TO CHANGE EXTERIOR LIFE

"How can I lift up my exterior life?"

"Lift up your interior mind."

"It is all so puzzling."

"Start by seeing that mind and life are one."

"I will try to see."

"Can you separate the nature of a buried seed from the kind of plant it produces above ground?"

"I see."

MIRAGE

"These teachings reject intellectualism, but what if all the best minds in the world could get together? Surely they could supply profound advice for solving our problems."

"When a thousand people with superb eyesight see a mirage it is still a mirage."

COLORFUL PACKAGES

"I am afraid to question my acquired beliefs."

"Don't be afraid to see that you have been cruelly deceived. A hungry man asked some officials for bread. With many smiles and sympathies they gave him several packages with colorful wrappings, assuring him he would never be hungry again. On the way home he could feel that the weight of the packages was not right for bread, so opening them, he found stones. Something in you can feel the difference between truth and falsehood, but you must courageously open the packages. You will then see how easy it is to throw away useless stones."

MENTAL MONEY

"By what method can I learn to think beneficially?"

"Think about your thinking. Your mind produces mental money. How do you spend it? Spend it for what you really need."

HONEST AWARENESS

"Today I noticed envy in myself."

"Good."

"Yesterday I became aware of resentment."

"Excellent."

"Excellent?"

"Of course. You are ending self-deception by becoming aware of your actual condition."

"But I seem to be getting worse."

"No, no, no! Honest awareness of your actual condition is the first step toward liberation from negative traits."

THINKING

"I have read hundreds of authoritative books and attended dozens of stimulating lectures. I now know what the great and famous teachers think."

"Yes, but what do *you* think?"

SINGLE MIND

"We are the victims of our own divided minds."

"You can give yourself a single mind which operates with clarity and power. Imagine a canvas ready for an artist's brush. But instead of a single artist, ten people step up in turn to add a few strokes of whatever they wish. One begins to paint a tree, another starts a cottage, and so on. You can imagine the hodgepodge on the canvas. Few people believe that their minds operate like this, yet their hodgepodge lives are perfect evidence."

"It makes me eager to have a single mind."

WORDS AND INSIGHT

"Last week we discussed the difference between hearing the words and having the insight. Please give us a practical project here."

"All hurt is self-hurt. Those are the words, now walk toward the insight."

"When will we fully understand this?"

"When heart knows what memory hears."

BURDENSOME THOUGHTS

"I am burdened by heavy thoughts about myself. How can I take myself less seriously?"

"By realizing that you are not at all the self you take so seriously."

THE JUNGLE

"You have stated that we must be willing to hear facts that we don't want to hear. Please give us one such fact."

"No man has a right to live according to his neurosis and then demand that others pay for the inevitable damage. It cannot be done anyway. Anyone attacked by jungle animals has first insisted upon wandering in the jungle."

"That is an interesting way of saying that we are indeed responsible for what happens to us."

THE WHOLE PICTURE

"What is a characteristic of a whole and healthy mind?"

"The ability to see the whole picture at once. Most people see only small parts, like looking at a famous painting which is mostly covered by a cloth. A healthy mind not only sees the whole painting but sees it instantaneously, as when the cloth is suddenly pulled off the painting."

HOW TO HAVE A HAPPY MIND

"How does wrong use of the mind make us unhappy?"

"Take any man. Year after year his mind flows along in a fixed stream. This customary flow includes two limiting and harmful assumptions. First, the man believes there is no way to think except his own. Secondly, he insists that others should think as he does, though this is never publicly admitted. You can see how his compulsive behavior and his angry demands make him unhappy. He must cease to be a limited stream to join the Whole Sea."

PEACE OF MIND

"How can I think peacefully toward both myself and others?"

"By learning the nature of thought itself."

"In what specific way?"

"Observe how every thought has an opposite. You want success, but fear failure. You feel elated, then depressed. You are arrogant one moment and cringing the next. This is conflict. Rise above thinking in opposites to the lofty level of mental wholeness. This is peace of mind."

"I have studied physical science for many years, never even dreaming of such an astonishing subject as mental science."

REMAIN HOME

"Please show us how to think with maximum benefit."

"End mental meandering. One hundred people applied for admission to a school of truth. They were told to go home and remain there until a messenger arrived who would inform them of time and place of the first class. On the first day of school, only three people entered. The rest had been absent when the messenger arrived, out making money or amusing themselves. Your mind can receive valuable messages every minute, but you must be home to yourself."

CHOICE

"Do we have a choice or do we not?"

"In his present mental confusion man is like a leaf blown up and down, left and right by every changing breeze. If a leaf thought like a man it would claim that it chose its own movements. Take a furious man or a dejected woman. Did they choose these feelings or were they blown into them by forces beyond their control?"

"Clearly, they have no choice. But can they change?"

"You can choose to turn yourself over to negative breezes or you can choose to not do so. Start with that. Later, everything else regarding choice will become clear."

BELIEFS AND FACTS

"You say we must replace human beliefs with cosmic facts, but what kind of a world will it be without beliefs?"

"What kind of a world is it *with* beliefs?"

USE THE RIGHT MENTAL TOOL

"How can we use the mind for right living in daily events?"

"By being in the right part of the mind at the right time. When driving your car, be attentive to driving; do not be lost in imagination. When meeting an unexpected event, do not react from stale memory, but see the event with a fresh mind which is unconnected with the past. Your mind is like a fully equipped kitchen that contains spoons, forks, and other cooking tools. In daily living, do not get your mental tools mixed up, but use the right tool."

THE BELL

"How can we expand our thinking?"

"By becoming aware of limited thinking. A visitor was inside a famous temple in Japan when its bell began to ring. The visitor asked the bell-ringer why the bell was sounding at this particular hour. The bell-ringer said it was because he was pulling on the rope. Limited thinking exists when one is able to see only visible causes."

REST YOUR MIND

"If we could just take a vacation from mental storms."

"These teachings show you how. There is something you must understand quite clearly. There is *thinking* and there is *seeing.* Thinking is necessary for daily tasks, but seeing is essential for psychic wholeness and the ease that goes with it. In this class you will learn how to alternate between practical thinking, as when cooking, and seeing, as when realizing that you need not seek approval from others. There are no storms in this natural alternation between thinking and seeing, so the mind is always at rest."

IMITATION INTELLIGENCE

"Last week in class you said that man lives from imitation intelligence. What did you mean?"

"A donkey desired to be as intelligent as his owner, so he decided to imitate his owner's ways. For three months the donkey stared at open books, just as he had seen his owner do. At the end of this time he prided himself on being highly intelligent. But he could never understand why he still had to bear burdens on his back."

PRACTICAL GUIDES

"I agree heartily that these teachings are the only practical guides on earth."

"Tell the rest of the class just how they have been practical."

"I was once helped to think for myself, instead of using the shallow ideas of others. I saw clearly the miserable results of letting other people think for me."

TRANSFORMED MIND

"I wish to escape my unhappy mind."

"Can you escape your own body?"

"No."

"Neither can you escape your own mind."

"Then my case is hopeless."

"Not at all. The mind cannot be escaped, but it can be transformed."

"How?"

"Cease to take a peculiar pleasure in thinking unhappy thoughts."

BOTHERATION

"I am bothered by what other people think of me."

"You have never been bothered by that. It is *your* thoughts about *their* thoughts that bother you. Now you know how to stop feeling bothered."

ACCURATE SOURCE

"When it comes to self-correction my problem is not a lack of advice, but too much of it. I look at everything I have been told and wonder what to do with it."

"A historian was researching the early days of Canada. He found so many errors in books about Canada's childhood that he decided to make correction. He did this by collecting original papers and documents. The assembled papers were left to speak for themselves. The historian refused to permit either himself or others to add opinions or guesses. To correct your life, go back to the original source of accuracy—your own clarified mind."

AUTHENTIC GUIDES TO SELF-NEWNESS

1. Worry ends by uplifting the level of cosmic insight.
2. Be aware of how thoughts create similar conditions.
3. Feel relief by realizing that there is a way out.
4. There is never a frantic need to prove oneself right.
5. Confusions fall away as we drop conditioned ideas.
6. Your own inner truth has total confidence in you.
7. Spend your mental money for what you really need.
8. Wisely replace dull human beliefs with cosmic facts.
9. A mind that has recovered its naturalness is at rest.
10. Be happily aware of the practical help of these guides.

Chapter 8

THE INSPIRING PATH TO REAL HAPPINESS

CHALLENGE THE CHAIN

"Please help us challenge the chain."

"A lion was captured. Around his neck was placed a chain which was tied to an iron stake. For awhile the lion submitted to captivity by accepting his daily food and never challenging the chain. But one day his lion nature rebelled at confinement, so he tugged mightily on the chain and stake. Observing this, his captors tried both promises and threats in an attempt to end the rebellion. But the lion refused to be fooled any longer. He broke the chain and escaped back to his natural ways."

BENEFICIAL LESSON

"From what do I suffer?"

"From what you do not know about yourself."

"I know that is right. You know, a few years ago I would not have been able to take what we hear in this group. I was hardened in my conceit. But my despair finally forced me to listen. It was a hard but beneficial lesson."

IMAGINARY LIFE

"I am dreadfully concerned with my life."

"The fact is you have never ever been concerned with your life. You are concerned with what you *imagine* is your life. You must see the difference in the two. Worry

126

over your physical appearance is imaginary life, as is concern with what others think of you."

"If I drop imaginary life, what is left?"

"*You.*"

HOW TO DROP SUFFERING

"The persistence of mental suffering baffles me. How can mental pain come to an end?"

"Stop glorifying suffering. It has no glory, not an ounce. Drop the secret and foolish self-glory in suffering and you will see it fall off like a dropped hat."

FALSE FEELING OF LIFE

"Several times you have mentioned a false feeling of life. Since some of us are new to these classes, may we have an explanation of this phrase?"

"A false feeling of life is a damaging substitute for true life. One lives in fiery thrills instead of from calm realities. It is as if an exploding volcano felt as alive as a human being. Take argument. If you let someone win every point in an argument he loses interest in the battle, for his excitement vanishes. If you wish to find true life, steadily reduce and finally eliminate false feelings of life."

OBSERVABLE SELF-TRANSFORMATION

"I have worked on myself according to these principles, but self-transformation eludes me."

"Work patiently on. A medical scientist can peer into a microscope to observe just how a medicine works upon and heals a human illness. He can actually see the change take place. Your inner transformation will become just as observable as you permit spiritual medicine to do what it is capable of doing."

WEAKNESS

"Maybe it is wrong, but I believe in my own weakness."

"Why? Truth doesn't believe in it."

FUNDAMENTAL FEAR

"What is the fundamental fear of man?"

"The fear that he does not exist as the kind of person he imagines he is. Suspecting that he is not this illusory person, he lives in anxiety and hostility, not knowing what else to do."

"The way in which we take illusion for reality and reality for illusion is becoming increasingly clear to me."

REAL PERSON

"How long must I suffer like this?"

"For as long as you prefer to play the role of a real person instead of finding out how to be one."

THE SECRET ROOM

"What about the disappointment felt upon self-examination?"

"Archeologists digging deeply into the ruins of ancient Athens were disappointed at their first discoveries. Expecting to uncover rare vases and other valuable objects, they found only cheaply made products. But with more digging, disappointment turned to delight. Below the worthless objects they discovered a secret room containing dozens of unique works of art. Those digging into their psychic systems will always uncover useless objects at first, but disappointment must be ignored. Keep digging. Beyond the worthless is the priceless."

CLIMBING THE HILL

"The blunders we make along the way!"

"Be like the man climbing the hill who took three steps upward to slide back one. What is wrong with that? You are still climbing."

REAL HAPPINESS

"How is real happiness attained?"

"By freeing yourself of thoughts *about* life. You have

thoughts as to how life should unfold, how people should treat you, how happiness can be won. These are your thoughts *about* life. But life cannot and will not obey your demanding thoughts, which makes you unhappy."

"But what can I do except think about life?"

"You can *see* life."

"How is this seeing attained?"

"By wanting seeing more than you want your demands upon life."

OBTAINMENTS

"I would be happy if I could just get what I want."

"How many times in the past have you obtained what you wanted?"

"Many times."

"Are you happy?"

HOW TO HEAR INNER HARMONY

"Why does a person fail to hear his natural inner harmony?"

"Because he stands too close to himself. Imagine yourself standing in the bell tower of a great cathedral in Europe. The bell rings, but you cannot hear its rich tones. You are too close, too confined. To hear and enjoy, stand at a distance."

"That connects with a lesson of last week. We learned of the existence of a special part of us capable of standing aside from our own confusion."

COMPLAINT

"Please discuss our many complaints."

"One of the most difficult facts for a complainer to grasp is his own involvement in the very game he complains so much about. He is a fox who insists he is a lamb. If he were not a part of the game he would not suffer from it. A complainer who sees this will emerge from suffering."

BE FEARLESS

"I fear what may happen to me."

"Who is this person with so many fears?"

"Pardon?"

"What you call your self is merely a hardened cluster of memories, labels, imaginations, vanities and identifications. You fear the ending of this illusory self, which is a false fear. Let go of what you call yourself and be fearless."

WANDERING MAN

"Sometimes it seems that I am hopelessly lost."

"No, you are merely wandering. When absent from home, is your home lost?"

DETACHMENT

"How can we remain untroubled while dwelling in a world of crimes and cruelties?"

"It is quite possible for eyes and ears to observe crimes and cruelties while being psychologically detached from their horrors. A person in this clear and lofty state does not contribute to the chaos. He is like a flower in a field of weeds."

SMOOTH WAY

"We want the smooth way."

"A smooth way consists of nothing but ceasing to be a problem to yourself. Some of you will resist this, for you still think from that part of the mind which wants to blame others for your own troubles. The smooth way appears with the willingness to listen to what you must learn."

"What must we learn?"

"To cease to be a problem to yourself."

VIEWPOINT

"Please discuss an error we must correct."

"A man mistakes his personal viewpoint of the world as the only world. This separates him from both himself and from the whole world. Imagine a motorist who has driven five miles beyond a bridge. Ask him where the bridge is and he will say it is five miles in back of him. But a second motorist going in the same direction is within five miles of reaching the bridge. He will state that the bridge is five miles ahead. So where is the bridge? Obviously it is in each man's personal viewpoint. Try to see that a personal viewpoint is not the only world."

WHAT IS RIGHT

"What is the difference between a true teacher and a false prophet?"

"A true teacher speaks only to what is right in you."

SELF-SLAVERY

"May we hear more about self-slavery? What is an example?"

"Pretending to be interested in something in which one has no real interest whatever. Impelled by self-interest, a man joins a club or cause which builds a flattering self-image of being a friendly and helpful member. But the man's secret despair knows better. This is one of the worst kinds of self-slavery, for it is so deeply hidden from whoever suffers from it."

"You didn't mean it that way, but you just described me."

HAPPINESS IN TRUTH

"When getting what I want I also get a quick thrill, but why does it fail to last?"

"Because life is movement and change."

"Why does the winning of my desires fail to create lasting happiness?"

"Because getting what you want leaves you the same kind of human being you were before."

"If I find happiness through an uplifted nature, will that happiness also change and fall away?"

"No. Happiness based in Truth does not change."

UNSEEN GOLD

"You once remarked that we never see all the gold in a simple lesson. What would be one such lesson?"

"Don't live as most people live. There is hidden gold in this short sentence. Among other things, it means you cannot admire successful but lost people, and it means you cannot label your borrowed ideas as original thinking."

MASKS

"What is the cause of and the cure for self-conflict?"

"A troubled man once came to a wrong conclusion. He concluded that the only way to go through life was to wear various masks. So he constructed clever masks to make him appear to be what he was not, which included a mask of happiness and a mask of confidence. After awhile, forgetting that they were mere masks after all, he began to believe he was actually happy and confident. This produced terrible self-conflict. Only when realizing what he was doing to himself did he put away both the masks and the conflict."

CONTENTMENT

"What is a sign of cosmic maturity?"

"The ability to be content when nothing exciting is happening."

LAW OF ATTRACTION

"I am bewildered and dismayed at what I attract into my life. This includes regretted actions and unwanted people. Why do I attract what I don't crave?"

"You attract what you really crave, not what you say you crave. But since this is unconscious, you don't accept it."

"I would like to stop attracting what I do."

"Then give up the false pleasure of your present cravings."

SUFFERING

"It almost seems that life wants us to suffer."

"Truth does not want anyone to suffer. It knows exactly how suffering can end, but truth also knows it must be welcomed by the sufferer."

"For many years I was about as receptive as a tree. I am changing all that."

ONENESS WITH EVERYTHING

"A particular happening bothers me constantly."

"Ask to whom it is happening. Do this. Inquire exactly who is the person bothered by the event. Carry the inquiry far enough and you will see that something is happening but not to you. In reality, you are not the feeling of botheration, but you take it as you, and so suffer from it. Deep knowledge of your true nature prevents happenings from becoming conflicts. This is a free state of oneness with everything."

THE OTHER SHORE

"How can we reach the other shore?"

"Two butterflies lived in a wild and dangerous region. One morning, when flying together, they came to a wide river. On the other side they could glimpse a land of peace and beauty. The first butterfly spoke up with several reasons why they should not fly over to the other shore. He said that the flight would be difficult, and that their miserable but familiar land was preferable to the new but unknown. The other butterfly said he had one strong reason for wanting to make the flight—he was thoroughly tired of living in a land of misery. With that declaration, he flew over to the other shore."

FRESHNESS

"What the world needs is spiritual freshness."

"For the bouquet to be fresh the flowers must be fresh."

FANTASIES

"You say that heartache is caused by mental fantasies. Would the ending of fantasies mean the ending of heartache?"

"Certainly. But you must see this as a fact through personal experience."

"How can I end fantasies?"

"By looking at them with full attention. This is a marvelous secret. You see, when looking at a fantasy you are apart from it for the moment, and therefore free of it."

RIGHT

"I need people to assure me that I am right."

"Why do you need to be right?"

"I will have to think about that unusual question."

THE FAMOUS LECTURER

"Please give us an incentive for finding the way out for ourselves, instead of depending upon authoritative personalities."

"A famous lecturer stood on the stage of a huge auditorium which was jammed with eager listeners. The lecturer assured them there was no need for failure, then supplied three easy rules for overcoming failure. He then told his audience that feelings of depression were completely unnecessary, then recited seven dynamic steps for victory over depression. As the lecture ended, the famous man was applauded enthusiastically. While driving home, the famous lecturer suddenly felt like a failure, which depressed him."

REASONS FOR UNHAPPINESS

"I am unhappy because life has denied me what I want."

"You are unhappy because of different causes than you imagine."

"Really?"

"You are unhappy because you are separated from yourself, not because you lack worldly success. You are anxious because you take the artificial as the real, not because your dreams did not come true. Remember always that you are unhappy for a different reason than you imagine. That will guide you all the way out."

SELF-QUESTIONING

"We are urged to question our habitual assumptions toward life. Obviously, that is a right move, but how can we do it?"

"You live by your own ideas as to what will attract happiness. Have your own ideas given you happiness? You live by your own choices as to what will make you feel secure. Have your choices provided security? You live by your own ambitions as to what will give meaning to your life. Have your ambitions made your life meaningful?"

BLEND WITH EVENTS

"I try to make events conform to my desires, but end up frustrated."

"Try building a fence around the wind. When you learn what it means to blend with events you will not know frustration."

"What does it mean to blend with events?"

"It means to no longer live from a separate self which is apart from events."

THE REVOLVING BIRD

"Beneath our pretenses we feel our uneasiness."

"Some workers in a Pennsylvania factory were inspecting some machinery at the top of a tower. They found a nest in a peculiar place. A bird had built its nest on a part of the machinery that slowly revolved day and night. No doubt the bird felt uneasy while in his nest, but did not know the cause. Men and woman feel vaguely uneasy in life, but do not know why. It is because they never really go anywhere. Meet a man again after twenty years and you meet the same man. Only awareness of going in circles can end it."

PERMANENT HAPPINESS

"I think I will be happy when something turns out as I wish."

"If you are happy because of *something,* you have artificial happiness which can vanish the next minute. A permanently happy person is one who is happy without knowing why. Now I will give you a work project. See how this connects with the virtue of psychological independence."

MUCH VALUE

"I do not know the answers."

"If the only thing you know is that the old ways are not the answers, you have already learned much of value. Keep going."

"The kind of encouragement we get here is genuine."

INFORMATION TO ACCEPT

"Why can't I make it?"

"Because you accept as a fact something which is not a fact. You accept your present life as all there is for you. Wrong. A small boy was asked his name. He said it was Tommy No. He had heard *no* so many times he had accepted it as part of himself. I now inform you that you can change yourself, which is the same as changing your life. Accept that information."

REAL OPTIMISM

"Man is making an effort to make this a better world."

"Effort based on concealed egotism and self-deception goes nowhere. Darkness cannot create light."

"But that is pessimism."

"Avoidance of the facts is the worst kind of pessimism, as well as dishonesty. What I am telling you is true optimism, for a sincere facing of the facts can change the facts."

THE JOINER

"I have joined dozens of social and religious organizations over the years, but remain as insecure as before."

"Join yourself."

THE ARGUERS

"I now see how dry intellectualism blocks self-renewal."

"No rain had fallen in a certain country for many months. The anxious officials consulted a wise man who told them to set out many buckets, for it would soon rain. But the officials remained actionless, arguing among themselves. Some insisted upon wooden buckets set out by men, while others demanded metal buckets to be set out by women. Consequently, the rain came and departed, leaving the country as dry as before. Now, you may imagine that they learned from this experience. Not at all. They did the same thing over and over and over."

COSMIC MELODY

"What is it like to sense this new world?"

"Imagine you had never heard music in your life, then suddenly heard a pretty melody. Everything within you would sense the newness of the experience. It is like that."

THE ZOO

"My inner life can be described as a howling zoo."

"There is a small part of you which is *not* part of the zoo. Diligent study of these principles permits this independent part to grow in size and strength."

''It seems that we really have but one task—to become clear to ourselves.''

ELATION AND DEPRESSION

''Why am I elated one day and depressed the next?''

''Because it is the nature of mechanical thought to swing back and forth in opposites. This includes elation and depression, like and dislike, attack and retreat. You want the elation without the depression, which is impossible, for both are sides of the same coin. In this class you will understand the falsity of both elation and depression, which lifts you above mechanical thought. Happiness resides on this higher level.''

REAL INDEPENDENCE

''You advise us to establish clear and definite aims. I have done this. I wish to be free of shallow attractions. I want to be independent of everyone and everything.''

''Reality loves a man who is indifferent to advantages, who declines favors.''

MISSING OUT

''I fear I may miss out on something life has to offer.''

''The fear of missing out is just another brick on the back. People with this burden really fear the ending of emotional excitement. To keep the thrill going they incite one emotional incident after another. That produces the fear of missing out. This is something an awakened man or woman never suffers from. Besides, a cosmically complete person never misses out on anything, any more than a sparrow misses the sky he flies through.''

DEVOTION

''We want to make it!''

''It has been estimated that a bee must visit fifty-thousand flowers to collect one pound of honey. Have that kind of devotion to the cause and you will make it.''

YOU WILL KNOW

"I try to become someone, but it wearies me."

"Why do you want to become someone?"

"Because I don't know who I am."

"Stop trying to know and you will know."

"That is unclear to me."

"Does an eagle try to become an eagle?"

GIVE UP DESPAIR

"Please speak frankly with us tonight."

"You cannot understand a condition and be free of it as long as you are in despair over it. Where despair rules, insight is absent. Liberty appears with a willingness to drop the despair of which you are so fond. Oh, yes, you love your despair for it makes you the star of your own little dramatic show. What I have just told you is not harsh and unfriendly. It is the beautiful truth that makes you free."

"Yes, we feel its rightness."

AUTHENTIC BOOK

"I wish to read a book of authentic guidance."

"How will you recognize its authenticity when seeing it?"

"I don't know."

"I will tell you what to do. By earnest self-exploration, develop one small authentic part within yourself. Then, when that authentic part comes across an authentic book there will be a meeting of two conscious items. Then, a bell of understanding will ring in your mind."

THE KITE

"I still don't see how I can get through my day without conflict."

"Like a kite. A kite soars and dips merrily because its nature does not oppose the changing winds. Being one with the entire sky, it has no opposition and therefore no conflict.''

''But we live in a warring world.''

''You are your own world.''

SOMETHING KNOWS

''Why should I walk the path?''

''Because nothing else in life is worthwhile.''

''But I do not know this.''

''Something within you knows it.''

TWO TIGERS

''What will be corrected as a result of our receptivity?''

''People just don't know how to behave in everyday situations. They don't know what to say or how to say it. They believe they must play a role, but worry that it might be seen through. They wonder whether it is good manners to accept a second slice of cake from the hostess. This kind of nervousness corrects itself. If you are tired of being caught between two tigers, give this some thought.''

STEADY GLOW

''The light seems to flicker.''

''If you have even a flicker of light you have cause for feeling fine. Be loyal to it. After awhile the flickering light turns to a steady glow.''

''May I say something? I am quite active in my business affairs, but these classes are the most important item in my schedule. Nothing matters but to know what life is really all about.''

INTERFERENCE

''I don't know what to do with my life.''

''Stop interfering with it.''

''In what way?''

''You tend a growing tree, but do you interfere with its natural growth?''

"No."

"Then stop interfering with your natural growth, for that makes you ask your original question. Stop seeking to be the tallest or most attractive tree. Stop interfering with what is right for *your* life."

NATURAL HEALING

"Tell us something about inner healing."

"It is a fascinating and natural process which can be felt as it goes along. To the degree that self-damage disappears through psychic understanding, self-healing appears. It is like the volcanic explosion on the island of Krakatoa in the last century. Trees, plants and grasses were utterly destroyed by the fierce blasts. But when the destruction ended, renewal began. Winds and tides carried the seeds of new life to Krakatoa, making it green again."

BE INSPIRED BY THESE REVELATIONS

1. We suffer only from a lack of self-knowledge.
2. The great quest in life is to become a real person.
3. Do not fear the ending of fantasies and illusions.
4. A wise man aims to cease to be a problem to himself.
5. Decide to not live in hidden anxiety as most people do.
6. Learn how to stop attracting unwanted experiences.
7. The basic cause of distress is separation from oneself.
8. A self-complete person never misses out on anything.
9. Something within you senses the majesty of the Path.
10. Do not interfere with what is right for your life.

Chapter 9

TREASURY OF PLANS FOR SELF-NEWNESS

THE HAPPY ROBIN

"How can we use unhappiness for needed schooling?"

"Feeling himself to be weak and inferior, a robin devised a way to attract attention and respect from other birds. He tied a whistle to his breast which sent out a fierce shriek as he flew along. The terrible sound did indeed attract a type of respect from other birds. But on one flight, to his horror, the whistle fell off, exposing his artificiality. The surface respect from the other birds turned to ridicule and rejection. But the robin took it as a lesson. He realized that he needed only to be what he was by nature—a free and happy bird."

OBSERVER ON A HILLTOP

"Whenever I see opposing sides on any social or political issue I never know which side to take."

"There is something far greater for you to know. It is the existence of a third position which takes no sides at all, for it is above human conflict. It is like standing on a hilltop and watching two battling armies. Such an observer does not contribute to the wounding of others."

DANGER

"I have noticed that teachings like these are often not given to those who need them most. Why?"

"A man who does not want to save himself from himself will not thank you for trying to save him."

"Such a man must remain a danger to himself."

"And to others."

"I am here to stop being a danger to myself."

THINKING HABITS

"You say it is good and necessary to break up our hardened thinking habits. Why?"

"Why does a farmer break up the ground before planting seeds?"

WONDER-WORKING QUESTION

"I cringe in despair over the flood of questions for which I have no answers."

"There is one wonder-working question you should ask."

"Tell me of it."

"Ask what is separating you from yourself. Answer that question, then see whether you have any other questions."

THE WITNESS

"What causes exciting but silly beliefs?"

"A combination of ignorance and a wish to be involved in sensational events. On a very dark night a rancher was making a minor repair on the roof of his barn. He dropped his lighted flashlight, which was caught by his son on the ground who tossed it back up. The incident was witnessed at a distance by a passing traveler. From that day forward the traveler solemnly told people that he had witnessed a miracle. He had, he said, actually seen a man jump from a barn roof to the ground and promptly jump back up."

SOMETHING WRONG

"We are urged to have kindness toward each other, which is certainly right. However, there is something wrong here, but I don't know what it is."

"Kindness without knowledge of human nature is not kindness at all, but an invitation to trouble. It is not a kindness to a wildcat to enter his cage to give him money."

THE LADDER

"I feel like I am living on a ladder that other people are always shaking."

"Have you ever asked yourself why you are climbing that ladder in the first place?"

SELF-ONENESS

"I wish to be one with myself."

"You are already one with yourself, however, this is hidden from you by wrong thoughts."

"What wrong thoughts?"

"Thoughts of being either successful or unsuccessful, thoughts of being good or bad, intelligent or stupid. Oneness is your natural state, but it can be seen only by rising above self-labeling thoughts."

SOCIAL CONTEST

"I must be a winner in the social contest."

"Why?"

THE RIGHT RING

"Why are we defeated in daily life?"

"A woman in a jewelry store examined a dozen rings on display. Excited over one ring in particular, she tried it on, but it was too tight. She tried to force it on, but the ring continued to resist her frantic efforts. She ended up feeling defied and defeated. Man invites vexation by insisting that attractive items should fit his demands."

"But is there a right ring for the woman?"

"Certainly, but she must drop her pointless obsession with that particular ring. And by the way, she will never tire of the ring that fits naturally."

HOW TO END NERVOUSNESS

"What can banish the nervousness that others might see through us?"

"See through yourself. Is this idea clear to you?"

"Yes. If I am not playing a role I can never be caught out of a role. What a simple but profound fact!"

PLEASANTLY ASTOUNDING

"You once predicted that these teachings would become more pleasantly astounding as we went along. You were right. I am thinking of a specific area. The exact opposite happens from what we thought would happen. Instead of being punished by the truth we are released from punishment."

"Yes, it is indeed a pleasantly astounding process. Take the act of letting go of stubborn ideas. The more you let go of yourself while fearing to do so the less afraid you become."

HAZARD

"You say that men and women live in hazardous illusions about themselves. After thinking it over, I don't think I live in illusion about myself."

"That is exactly what makes it so hazardous."

SOCIETY'S SITUATION

"It is obvious that something higher than society must supply the cure for society."

"Society is unable to recognize its own illness except when it appears in an extreme and visible form, as with an obviously disturbed person who wanders out into a busy street. But an awakened man sees through so-called normal people, being fully aware of their buried terrors and compulsions. But society cuts itself off from his help by a second nonrecognition—its inability to recognize his profound insight."

ACCEPT THE NEW!

"We seem to cut ourselves off from what we really need."

"Yes. Man fears and rejects the new and unknown which could save him from himself. A party of scholars prided themselves on speaking every language in the land. While traveling together over a mountain they heard a few citizens speaking in a strange tongue. With wounded vanity they accused the mountain dwellers of using a nonsensical and even traitorous language. They never learned that this new and dynamic language could have taught them to live without pride and vanity."

ANOTHER WORLD

"For long enough I have been trying to make sense out of nonsense. It is time to stop."

"It is nice, is it not, to be among members of this group who have the same aim?"

"It is like living in another world."

"It *is* another world."

"Yes, I feel it."

PRACTICAL

"These lofty ideas may have their place, but this is a practical world. We must live as practical human beings."

"Do you fear what other people can do to you?"

"Sometimes."

"*That* is what you call practical? Do you sometimes burn yourself with suppressed resentment?"

"Yes."

"*That* is your practical way? Learn what it really means to be practical."

WRONG INNER STATES

"What wrong inner states do beginners often have?"

"They yearn to ask personal questions about the pri-

vate life of the teacher, but dare not. They play the foolish game of ego-competition with the teacher, not realizing
that he is not playing the game at all. They expect clever
jokes and dazzling dramatics from the teacher, turning
sour and critical when he gives them truth instead. Before
a beginner can become a learner, all such immaturity must
go.''

FIND OUT

''Everything goes against me.''
''Who is this *me* you speak about?''
''I don't know.''
''Find out, and nothing will go against you.''

COMPETENT MANAGER

''Since not everyone wants the message that an awakened man has to give, how does he know which ones to
teach?''

''He knows. Seeing through human nature, he easily
distinguishes between those who pretend to want the truth
and those who really do. He can be compared with a competent hotel manager. Five guests in the hotel ask to be
called at six in the morning. Five other guests say they do
not want to be disturbed at any time. The manager knows
who to call and who to leave alone. But a man who merely imagines he is awake makes mindless blunders. Getting
his lists mixed up, he calls the wrong people and gets into
trouble.''

RIGHT FEELINGS

''Everyone wants to feel right, but nothing we do attracts right feelings.''

''The solution is so simple that few ever see it.''

''Are you saying that we miss the obvious?''

''We choose what is popular instead of what is right and
then wonder why we don't feel right.''

HOW TO FIND A NEW WAY

"Why is my way so hard?"

"Because you are hard."

"What does that mean?"

"It means that you and your way are the same thing. Change yourself and you change your way.There is no other way."

PAST FOLLIES

"I would like to ask about something that has puzzled me for the last month. You say we can be free of the past. But how can it be so? Past follies are like wolves inside our minds. Every few days they leap out to attack us."

"The past can exist in your memory without affecting the present moment, for you do not live in time; you live only in Now. See this, and the illusory power of the past falls away."

"You know, I was afraid to ask that question."

"For fear there might not be an answer?"

"Right!"

THE HYPNOTIZED LAMB

"It is painful to be at the mercy of exterior events."

"A lamb was hypnotized by some evil wolves and was told a peculiar falsehood. They made him believe he would be happy when the wind blew westward, but would be sad when the wind blew eastward. The innocent lamb accepted this nonsense without question. So not only did he suffer half the time, but felt helpless and irritable at having lost control of his own feelings. But he studied his condition until seeing through the hypnotic hoax. Then awakened, he knew his inner happiness was independent of exterior winds."

ARTIFICIAL BEHAVIOR

"As you have pointed out, artificial behavior is exhausting. We would like to end it."

"You must first see the difference between artificial and natural behavior."

"How can we do this right here in class?"

"Do not try to please me in order to make me pleased with you."

DEEP FACT

"Please give us a particularly deep and helpful fact."

"When saying that a man has no conscience, how does the mind react? In almost every case it thinks that the man has no conscience toward other people, that is, he is cruel and deceitful to others. That is true, but only one person in ten million can see deeper than that. That rare person sees that *the conscienceless man also has no conscience toward himself.* He is not divided into two people, one of them kindly to himself and the other heartless toward others. His lack of conscience punishes himself at the same instant it injures others, though he rarely sees it."

SELF-FINDING

"Daily life is so dull."

"Try finding yourself. Nothing is more fascinating."

CURE FOR THE INDIVIDUAL

"This class has helped me see something startling but valuable about certain social involvements. I used to think they gave me something, but now I see how they drained the energy needed for constructive living."

"Your experience is quite characteristic of those who attend to their lessons. What you believed was a diamond was seen to be a mere pebble."

"I also see why self-study alone can cure the individual. Your patience with my fumbling efforts is appreciated."

OUT OF THE CAVE!

"Is it really possible to find my own way out?"

"It becomes possible the moment you suspect you have been misled by other people. By making up a story of hidden treasure, some cunning robbers persuaded some strangers to enter a deep cave. The thieves intended to rob and abandon the strangers. But one stranger became suspicious, so he quietly marked the wall of the cave as they passed from one dark branch to another. In a moment when the robbers were inattentive, the wise stranger slipped away and followed his own marks all the way out of the cave.''

WEARINESS

''What is essential to genuine self-transformation?''

''One must be utterly weary of his present ways.''

''Then I qualify. I am utterly weary.''

''Then come to the class tonight to hear about the way out.''

''But there is something else I want to do tonight.''

''Your weariness is not directed toward self-transformation, but toward self-escape.''

MOUNTAIN AND DESERT

''I would like to talk with more people about this new way, but it is difficult to communicate with them.''

''You always come back to the same problem. You cannot tell a man who does not know that he does not know. You cannot even tell him that he does not know that he does not know. He cannot hear you. Suppose a mountain rabbit described snowy peaks to a desert rabbit. Could the desert rabbit comprehend?''

''Still, there is a way out, for some have found it.''

''Yes—those who declined to accept the false pleasure of emotional agitation.''

ALLIES

''From this higher viewpoint, what is a wrong position?''

''Any position requiring allies is a wrong position, even if those allies are friends and relatives. The man who *knows from himself* needs no allies at all. By the way, such a truly independent man is free from quarrels, for allies always end up battling each other.''

RIGHT RECEPTACLE

''How can we stop attracting adversity?''

''Let your mind be a right receptacle for offered truths. A citizen of a hot and dry country owned a well having an abundance of water. A generous man, he hung a sign over the well which invited weary travelers to freely fill their jugs. Over the years the citizen observed a tragic fact. The jugs of some of the travelers were too small, others leaked, while still others were too frail. He knew their journey would be difficult, for they had faulty receptacles.''

EVERYTHING CAN BE DONE

''Something you said in the last class made a deep impression on me. I have been thinking about it all week. You said that nothing can be done for someone who refuses to listen, but that everything can be done for whoever simply listens.''

''Yes, that is one of those plain facts with a deeper meaning than appears on the surface.''

''We must get tired of listening to our own nonsense, then maybe we will listen to the rescuing facts.''

UNNECESSARY BLOCKAGE

''Sometimes I feel that the task is too difficult.''

''Why do you permit a mere word to stand in your way? Forget the word *difficult* and take your next step.''

IMAGINARY FREEDOM

''I am sure I possess this freedom you teach.''

''No. You only imagine it.''

''How do you know?''

''Yesterday you talked with some nervous strangers.''

"That is right."

"I observed you."

"And?"

"Anxious people can still make you anxious."

EAGLES AND PARROTS

"There seems to be an absence of real teachers."

"That is because of the absence of real students."

"It is obvious that careless people will follow almost anyone who claims to have the answers."

"There was a country which had no eagles, so parrots were called eagles."

THE ORCHESTRA

"We talk a lot about human harmony, but where is it?"

"The conductor of a symphony orchestra instructed his musicians to prepare to play a certain composition. Accordingly, the musicians placed the needed music on their stands. At the signal from the director the orchestra played—a horrible blast, shocking to ears. What went wrong? Each musician played his own preferred selection. While pretending to be part of the harmonious whole, each man actually played his secret and self-centered preference. That is why talk about human harmony is just talk. And that is why mankind suffers from shocking blasts."

PLANS

"My plans seldom work out."

"Individual plans do not exist. Everything is a movement of the Cosmic Whole, which includes you."

"But sometimes I get what I want."

"Pure coincidence. But you take it as personal success and set yourself up for the next knockdown."

"That is startling, but it rings true."

BREAKTHROUGH

"Somewhere along the line I need to make a breakthrough."

"Understand what I am about to tell you and there will be a major breakthrough. You are never made unhappy by a result that goes contrary to what you wanted. *You are made unhappy by your very love of being negative over the result.* You love and value the false feeling of life supplied by frustration. If you did not love feelings of frustration you would never be frustrated by anything."

QUALITIES THAT COUNT

"How can we start to possess qualities that count?"

"There is only one right start. We must stop attributing qualities to ourselves and to others which do not in fact exist. Calling an artificial pearl a real pearl prevents knowledge of the real gem."

FACTS ABOUT SELF-TEACHING

"Do I need a teacher, or can I teach myself?"

"Suppose you attend a class to learn to speak French. But other students want to learn Spanish, German, Dutch and other languages. Wishing to please everyone in order to get his fees, the teacher gives you only an occasional word of French. But even this is worthless, for you cannot as yet distinguish between French and the other languages. So you must teach yourself until getting some idea of the nature of French. Then when meeting an authentic and conscientious teacher, your own knowledge will reveal his authenticity and you will want to learn from him."

PRESENCE AND ABSENCE

"How can we tell just where we are living in illusion?"

"Presence of pain, presence of illusion. Absence of pain, absence of illusion."

BOREDOM

"I am bored. I want another life."

"No, you don't want another life; you want a new toy. When you really want another life, bring me your toys.

And by the way, a toy can range from a weekend activity to governing an empire.''

EASY QUESTION

''I find it hard to believe that we can answer our own questions.''

''Start with an easy question. Are you a free man or are you not?''

''I don't know.''

''Do you become angry and depressed?''

''Sometimes.''

''Are you a free man or are you not?''

MESSAGE OF WONDERS!

''Please discuss the need for earnest attention.''

''At one of our national parks there is a building which supplies information for visitors. When the building is closed, visitors can press a button and hear a recorded message which describes the natural wonders of the region. I once saw some playful children push the button and run away. Doesn't that remind you of most human beings? They really don't want to listen to truth; they just want to play around.''

''And they never know the wonders they have missed.''

REAL GOODNESS

''You have said that real goodness has a cunning counterfeit. So how can we distinguish between cosmic goodness and the artificial version?''

''False goodness always attracts a negative reaction. For instance, the next time you generously contribute your time and energy to others, observe whether you secretly resent it. This indicates that the so-called generosity was merely a trading game. You gave perhaps to feel approved by others, or maybe to relieve a conditioned sense of guilt. Remember that artificial goodness always feels burdened, while true goodness is effortless.''

THE QUESTION

"I am what I am. Why am I punished for it?"

"No, no. You are punished *by* it."

"Then why am I punished by it?"

"No, no. The question is, why do you prefer to remain what you are."

GIVING

"I wish to give something to the world."

"What do you have to give?"

"What I possess."

"What you possess is the same as what you are. What are you?"

"I see what you mean."

COME OUT OF HIDING

"What is the aim of an awakened man?"

"To call frightened people out of hiding. A cruel warrior once led his savage troops in an invasion of a weak nation. The terrified citizens fled to caves in distant mountains. They became so accustomed to cave-life that they refused to return home, even when assured that it was safe to do so, for the warrior had departed. An awakened man calls at mental caves, urging everyone to come out of hiding and return home. Unfortunately, his good news is ignored by many people."

SOCIETY'S SUBSTITUTE

"If only people would love each other more!"

"Every time society uses the word *love* it flatters and deceives itself into thinking it knows the meaning of love."

"What stands in the way of love?"

"Society's substitute of the word for the virtue."

NEW EXPERIENCE

"I need something, but do not know what."

"What you need are new experiences."

"What is a new experience?"

"How will you react the next time you are blamed for something? I know and you know how you will react, for you are always the same. You will react with anxiety, defensiveness, hostility. A new experience would be to take the blame without feeling disturbed, without a tense ego-reaction."

"What is the value of this?"

"What is the value of being without anxiety and hostility?"

HEAVENLY DIAMOND

"Why are there so many conflicting religions?"

"An angel appeared to a group of men and showed them a brilliant diamond. After telling them that the heavenly diamond would be left in a secret place on earth, the angel disappeared. Immediately, the men formed rival groups which battled each other over what they had witnessed. One group claimed to be the exclusive earthly representative of the angel. Another group tried to attract believers by putting on a stage show about a heavenly diamond. But no one ever thought of trying to find the diamond itself."

PERFUME

"I know why you said we must study the artificiality of human life here on earth."

"Why?"

"Because an artificial flower has no perfume."

SUPREME UNDERSTANDING

"Please guide us on the matter of seeking help."

"While help can certainly come from those who have found the way out for themselves, you must also remember the foremost fact about help. There is no final help outside your own understanding, and no need for any, for your recovered understanding is supreme."

THOUGHT TO CONSIDER

"May we have a thought to consider on the way home?"

"One thing above all prevents the entrance of the remedy. It is the wish to hear the pleasing instead of the healing."

"You have clear insight into human ways."

THE COLUMBINE

"I have heard that these esoteric teachings are kept secret. Still, they seem openly available. How can they be both secret and open?"

"Twelve men took a stroll in the springtime countryside, abundant with colorful flowers. Hidden among the dozens of different kinds of flowers was a single columbine. Only one man out of the twelve recognized and appreciated the one columbine. Why? Because he was the only man with an intense interest in flowers. Now, was that columbine a secret or was it out in the open?"

SUMMARY OF PLANS FROM THIS CHAPTER

1. Wrong thoughts alone cut us off from our true good.
2. Living in truth is like living in another world.
3. Nothing ever goes against a self-enlightened man.
4. Follow your natural intelligence all the way out.
5. Whoever really knows the Answer needs no allies.
6. Be a right receptacle for cosmic refreshment.
7. Remember always that here is the message of wonders.
8. Truth tries to call frightened people out of hiding.
9. Your recovered understanding is the supreme teacher.
10. These noble secrets are open to all who seek them.

Chapter 10

ROYAL ADVENTURES ALONG THE WAY OUT

SAFE HARBOR

"If only our psychic hearing were better!"

"In earlier days of sailing, a large fleet of cargo ships was traveling together across the South Pacific. A sudden storm caught the fleet, damaging and scattering the ships. One of the vessels managed to locate and limp into the harbor of an island, where repairs could be made. The captain of the safe ship sent a radio message to the ships still dazed by the storm. He urged them to join him in the harbor. But only those ships having a radio receiver could hear the message and accept the invitation."

PRACTICAL HELP

"Please suggest a way to use these principles for practical help in daily affairs."

"When a difficulty arises, instantly remember one of the guides learned in class. When feeling depressed, remember that depression is simply a mental movie which can be broken off with consciousness. When fearful of losing something, remember that your real nature cannot suffer any kind of loss. Remember!"

WHAT MAN SUFFERS FROM

"Would you say that a person's unhappiness is caused by the number of things he cannot obtain?"

"No, no. His unhappiness is caused by the number of

things he cannot be told. He really suffers from what he cannot be told because of defensiveness, hardness, fear, vanity, ignorance.''

''If we could only get out of our own way.''

THE WAY OUT!

''Is there really a way out?''
''Yes.''
''Can you show it to me?''
''Yes.''
''What must I do?''
''Listen patiently to facts you don't want to hear.''

THE BRIDGE

''One part of us wants self-change, but another part resists.''

''I will tell you what man is like. He is like a small child who glimpses several children at play on the other side of a high bridge. The child gazes longingly over, wishing to join the happy activities. But at the same time that he sees the other side he also sees the bridge—which he fears to cross. Do you know what a true teacher is? He is someone who has crossed the bridge himself. He can therefore assure you that in spite of all your fears it is perfectly safe to cross the bridge.''

HEALING FACT

''Help us to distinguish between fantasy and fact.''

''Falsehood often sounds pleasant, but leads to dismay. Truth may sound displeasing, but it carries you forward. See that very clearly. See it so clearly that it becomes impossible to prefer deceptive fantasy to healing fact.''

SOCIAL DRAMA

''I want to give up my role in the absurd social drama.''
''To do that you must clearly understand the drama.''
''How is that accomplished?''

"Simply by stepping offstage to observe it."

"I think I see what you mean."

"You cannot really comprehend the drama as long as you are part of it."

"But why does one part of me love the foolish dramatic role?"

"It loves the applause."

THE ARTIST

"Suppose a troubled individual wants the help of a man who really knows the answers. How can he proceed?"

"Do you remember the rule explained in a previous class? You cannot receive value from a man who knows unless you have at least a faint recognition of his knowledge. A famous Japanese artist took a leisurely journey around the country, seeking interesting scenes to sketch. Though carrying his art supplies openly, he never revealed his identity. When stopping at an inn for the night he offered to pay the innkeeper with either money or with a new drawing. Only those innkeepers who recognized the artist were wise enough to take the drawing."

THE ALARMED BIRDS

"For the first time I am quite aware of how we misinterpret the approach of healing facts."

"When approaching birds with bread crumbs they fly away in alarm, quite sure you mean to harm them. People are no different."

"I used to run away like that. No more."

WHERE YOU REALLY ARE

"How can I find God, Truth, Reality?"

"By doing one thing at a time, slowly while being aware of yourself doing it."

"How does this help me find Reality?"

"It breaks off the habitual and mechanical and unconscious movements of mind and body. It is these unconscious movements which separate you from Reality. A man riding a recklessly galloping horse is in a beautiful meadow, but cannot see it. By commanding the horse to slow down he sees where he is. In the same way this technique shows you where you really are—in union with Reality.''

DISSATISFACTION

''I am dissatisfied.''

''It can take you up or down.''

''Depending upon what?''

''Upon whether you use it to complain or to learn.''

SELF-MIRACLE

''May we hear more about an idea you mentioned briefly yesterday? You spoke of a self-miracle.''

''You can make yourself a miracle. This is not said to make you excited or make you feel good. It is said because it is a fact. I know it is a fact. You can know it from your own personal experience. A self-miracle happens when you face what you don't want to face so long and so bravely that the very facing changes the kind of human being you are. Make yourself a miracle.''

MAN'S WORST ENEMY

''Please explain how a man becomes his own worst enemy.''

''A traveler found himself stranded in an oasis. It was an unpleasant place, but he saw a chance to make quick profits. One well in the oasis supplied a trickle of pure water, while another well flowed with impure water. He gave samples from the pure well to passing travelers, assuring them that their waterbags would be filled with the same healthy water. But once receiving payment he substituted the impure water. He became wealthy. But one day the pure water ceased to trickle, so he himself had to drink from the unhealthy well.''

SUCCESSFUL DAY

''What is the difference between a man who is not rescuing himself and one who is?''

"The lost man calls his day successful when no one has seen through his staged roles and his pretenses. The self-rescuing man calls the day successful when he has detected and dropped one of his enslaving roles."

"I have waited a long time to hear that."

BE MORE DARING!

"We are urged to be more daring toward our liberation. Please show us how."

"Dare to be without something to do. People would be shocked to see how many activities they invent out of fear of having nothing to do."

"And probably dismayed at the worthlessness of most of them. But what is behind our fear of inactivity?"

"Exciting but useless activities are similar to certain kinds of birds which shriek and leap in an attempt to lead an enemy away from the nest. Man's artificial movements are his attempts to hide his pretenses of being wise and important."

DISTRACTIONS

"I now see how we distract ourselves from our own good."

"An ill man was walking down the street when he came to a shop selling just the medicine he needed. Refusing to enter the shop he continued down the street. He finally came to a toy shop which he entered to make several purchases. See the point? Those who refuse the medicine accept the toys."

HAZARDOUS CAUSES

"Why do I have painful experiences again and again?"

"Because your memory is too short. You put the same hazardous causes into motion while dreaming that the results will be different. They won't."

"What are these hazardous causes?"

"Your inner characteristics, the ones you keep hidden from yourself and others."

THE SENSIBLE MAN

"How can we escape the self-storm?"

"By realizing fully that you are caught in it. Imagine a man sleeping under a blanket in the woods. A thundering storm suddenly crashes over his head. If sensible, he will jump up and race out of the woods."

"But how can we feel this urgency?"

"One part of you feels it all day long, as when caught in gloom and irritation. But another part hides under the blanket and pretends there is no storm."

"That is the part we will work on."

EXPERIENCES

"Our study group meets next Saturday. May we have an idea for discussion?"

"You always get what you ask for, for you *are* what you ask for. In the psychological world there is no division between what you are and what you get. A donkey gets the experiences of a donkey because it is a donkey. A lion gets the experiences of a lion because it is a lion."

OFFERED ADVICE

"I now see the folly of accepting all offered advice."

"Yes. It is useless to ask a poor man to describe pearls."

EASY CURE

"I wish to learn more about the cause of my problems."

"Imagine yourself watching a number of shadows leaping around against a wall. But from your limited viewpoint you cannot see whether they are caused by people or birds or branches. Only by shifting to another position can you discover the cause of the shadows. These teachings place you in new viewpoints which reveal the actual cause of personal difficulties. Then, the cure is easy."

EXERCISE IN CLARITY

"Will you please repeat an exercise you gave us last week? You said it is helpful to state the same idea in different ways."

"No experience has real value unless it leaves you with something you did not know about yourself before. Now say the same thing another way. You might say that every experience providing a lesson about yourself is valuable. Next, think of a third version. An idea becomes clearer by stating it in different ways. Practice this either mentally or by writing down the various versions of the same idea."

HARMFUL BEHAVIOR

"What is a kind of self-harming behavior we rarely notice?"

"Self-dramatization."

"Why is it harmful?"

"How do you feel when the show is over?"

SLOW DOWN AND THINK

"I am surprised that I didn't see things long before now. But now I know why. I was asleep, dreaming that I was awake."

"What was your turning point?"

"It came gradually, but there were special moments. One time you said we had to stop chasing around in a frantic effort to convince ourselves of happiness. I realized that I was making that very mistake. It helped me to slow down and think about my life."

FLOWERS

"Show us one way in which man has gone wrong."

"The citizens of a large country wanted to grow flowers, but did not know how to make them grow in their barren soil. As a substitute they constructed artifical flowers made out of paper and glue. The artificial flowers were so cleverly constructed that they became a great commercial success. Orders for them poured in from around the globe. One day a visiting botanist offered to show the people how to grow real flowers, even in their barren soil. But the citizens were disinterested. They were too busy getting rich. They much preferred artificial flowers to real blossoms!''

HOW CHANGE OCCURS

''Why do I do what I do?''

''You do what you do because you do it. That is all.''

''Please explain.''

''At the exact moment that you do something, you and your motive are the same thing. There is no you *and* a motive. At that precise moment you *are* your motive. This is quite deep, so I will summarize for now. You can change what you do only by dropping the illusion of having a separate self which can change what you do. Change occurs only in the absence of the imaginary self.''

SEE FOR YOURSELF

''Teach us something we need to know.''

''I will give you a liberating lesson which at first you may take as unpleasant nonsense.''

''We are listening.''

''You think that the world revolves around you. Yes, each of you actually believes himself to be the center of everything on earth. And you think it all day long.''

''Why is this a liberating lesson?''

''Stop thinking it and see for yourself.''

GOD

''Do you believe in God?''

''You have used the word *God,* so we must see what you mean by it. Everyone has a different explanation. So when you say *God,* what do you mean?''

''Now that you ask, it is difficult to answer.''

''The word is not the thing. The word *apple* is not an

apple. Go beyond the word to personal experience, then you will understand God.''

NIAGARA FALLS

''I have helped myself just by seeing how much help I must give myself.''

''That is a good attitude. I will give you something to work on. Remember that repression is not conquest. An angry man who pushes his anger down is still an angry man. A strange thing once happened to Niagara Falls. It stopped falling. Huge blocks of ice formed a dam on the river above the falls. Then, one spring morning the great pressure forced the ice aside, releasing an explosion of water downstream. This pattern of repression and explosion is so common in human conduct.''

''We want liberty, not suppression.''

DELIGHT

''What a tragedy when all a man has is what he has on the outside.''

''What a delight when he makes that first small inner change that changes his outer life effortlessly.''

LIBERATING FACT!

''People alternate between two moods. They are either darkly depressed or they act out an artificial cheerfulness which fools no one. According to these teachings, there is a third way.''

''There is indeed. It is the way of freedom. A person feels depressed when his illusory ideas about himself are shattered. Or, he feels elated when his self-ideas seem affirmed. For example, it is a false idea that you must appear successful to others. You need have no ideas about yourself whatever. Instead, know yourself as part of the Cosmic Whole. That is not an idea, but a liberating fact.''

GIVING AND RECEIVING

''How can we get rid of feelings of darkness?''

''By living above the level which both sends out and receives darkness. Some factory workers in Belgium complained about black smoke coming into a window. Investigation proved that the smoke was coming out of another window in the same factory. You receive whatever you send.''

''But people deny that they send out darkness.''

''Denial changes nothing. Honesty alone can change anything.''

THE MAP

''Unfortunately, people seem to arrange their lives according to pleasures and preferences, not according to realities.''

''Yes, and then are so indignant when things go wrong! A boy asked a young friend to draw a map of some woods with which the friend was acquainted. When using the map a day later the boy became temporarily lost in the woods. The cause was an incorrect map. A stream flowed where a path was indicated, and thick bushes covered ground where a field was supposed to be. When the boy questioned his friend about it the friend replied that he had drawn the woods the way he wanted them to be, not as they were. Does that remind you of some people?''

ENCHANTMENT

''These facts are both enchanting and baffling. Please explain a baffling one. You say that anyone can free himself of feeling attacked and injured. How?''

''Attack the air with a stick. Nothing happens because the air is of a different nature than the stick. Dissolve your present nature. There is no one left to feel hurt.''

''Now we are enchanted.''

WORSHIP

''Please tell us about worship.''

''False worship exists where there is division, that is, where there is a worshipper and whoever is worshipped. This worship enables the worshipper to cling to his illusion of having an ego apart from the Whole. He wrongly believes there is a self *and* the object of his worship. This is both vanity and idolatry, for the worshipper is simply praising his own personal ideas about the object of his worship. In true worship, there is only Oneness, so even the word *worship* has no significance.''

COSMIC ATMOSPHERE

''It is interesting how right thoughts are followed by right feelings. It makes me want to travel all the way.''

''The greater the distance a boat travels from land, the purer the air. You breathe and feel a fresh psychological atmosphere. Give a voyager a breath of cosmic air and he will never turn back to the old land.''

FEELING OF RELEASE

''One of the strongest impressions I ever received in this class occurred the night you spoke about artificial duties. Just hearing about the way we needlessly burden ourselves inspired a feeling of release.''

''A careless man let himself be hypnotized into believing it was necessary to carry a heavy rock on his back during the day. He believed that failure to carry the rock would make him a guilty or lazy person. So he dutifully and resentfully placed the rock on his back every morning before leaving home. So living from an imaginary self creates imaginary obligations.''

''We want to snap out of the hypnosis!''

OPINIONS AND FACTS

''We are urged over and over to drop acquired opinions. But this would leave us without a steering wheel.''

''Where has your steering wheel taken you up to now?''

''But what would I be without strong opinions?''

''A real person. You mistake opinions for facts without realizing you are doing so. The only way to obtain liberating facts is to first drop enslaving opinions.''

HOW ANXIETY FADES

"One idea supplied several months ago helped me considerably. You summarized man's problem to himself. It is his incapacity to listen to anything beyond his rigid assumptions as to what is right. As I have dropped fixed assumptions, I have noticed the lessening of anxiety."

"Yes. Anxiety fades. It resembles the beat of a drum that falls at longer and longer intervals until disappearing altogether."

WISH TO UNDERSTAND

"When pained people seek help at a truth-lecture, where do they make a mistake?"

"People come with a desire to get rid of the pain, but not with a wish to understand. No greater blunder could be made, for pain ends only through understanding. To reach higher understanding it is necessary to pass through the valley of ego-humiliation, which most people refuse to do. Therefore they continue to alternate between pain and a temporary escape into daydreams."

"The trouble with escaping into dreams is that reality is always shaking us awake."

HIGHER LEVEL

"In what way is an awakened man on a higher level than I?"

"You *think*. He *sees*."

THE MARVELOUS BOAT

"What prevents us from learning from a man who knows?"

"Wrong attitudes toward him. A seaman built a small boat for himself which was the marvel of the harbor. It sailed with the smallest breeze. The skilled seaman was willing to teach others to build their own marvelous boats, but few ever asked for his instructions. Some wanted to substitute their own ideas, while others simply asked for a ride in the seaman's boat. Some people plainly showed envy, while some faint-hearted builders gave up shortly after starting. But the few who really wanted to learn soon had their own marvelous boats.''

FUTURE

''What is my future?''

''Your nature is your future. The simplest of logic reveals that your nature must repeat itself tomorrow. The one way to change your future is to change your nature. But you must really change it, and not merely imagine that you are different.''

''Thanks to this class I am becoming more aware of how imagination masquerades as reality.''

GREAT SECRET

''The world is so overwhelmed with anxiety.''

''Yes, but a great secret exists for the earnest individual. Instead of merely suffering from anxiety he can study it. See the simple difference?''

''Yes. It is obvious that only the facts can save us.''

''Of course, but how many people want to face the facts? It is like the woman who kept reading that too much candy was bad for her health, so she gave up reading.''

PERSONAL MANUSCRIPT

''I am trying to see how I cause my own experiences.''

''An ancient manuscript was discovered in a dungeon of a castle in the Rhineland. At first the author's identity was unknown, but close inspection of the last page disclosed the writer's name. Close examination of individual urges and motives disclose that the individual himself is the author of whatever happens to him. He writes his own life-manuscript.''

COSMIC COMMUNICATION

''How is cosmic consciousness communicated?''

''It happens only under unique circumstances. Precisely,

it occurs when a man who knows meets a man who wants
to know. Cosmic communication results, as though a ray of
light appeared between them."

"But how can an ordinary man experience this?"

"You are already an extraordinary man if you really
want to know. This ardent wish will lead you to someone
who knows."

CHANGE OF CIRCUMSTANCES

"If I am deceiving myself I want to know about it."

"You still believe that a change in circumstances will
make you happy. How little you understand. Surround a
bored man with exciting activities and he will soon be bored
again. Give a frustrated man everything he demands and
his frustration will remain to torture him. Only a profound
change in the way we think can make us happy."

SELF-DIVISION

"You urge us toward self-union? What is self-division?"

"There was once a rich and powerful nobleman who was
envied and admired by everyone. One day a poor man accidentally wandered on to the private grounds of the nobleman. With angry threats the rich man ordered the poor man
away. From that day forward the poor man never again
envied or admired the rich man. The poor man understood
self-division. He knew it meant to appear in public to be
worthy of praise, but to be the private slave of rage."

DYNAMIC SENTENCES

"I have written down several dynamic sentences which
have impressed me during the last few classes. Maybe they
would interest others."

"Please read them aloud to us."

"Never permit anyone to impose a sense of guilt upon
you. A negative man provokes negativity in others and then
wonders why he is surrounded by negative people. Saying
we want correction and taking correction are two different

things. There is no truth whatever in fiery argument. All is well for the earnest person, for the Answer exists."

QUESTIONS AND ANSWERS

"I am utterly weary of asking so many baffling questions."

"Wonderful! Now you can listen to enlightening answers."

THE BUILDER

"Why are we afraid? What is the cure?"

"A man began to build a house. Because he lazily refused to obtain knowledge about his work he built the house with faulty materials. The higher the house rose the more fear he felt. One day, in a moment of great decision, he abandoned the house to start a new one with reliable materials. His fear vanished."

TRUTH

"What is meant by the word *truth?*"

"Truth is anything that helps you to become a different kind of person than you now are. It is truth to explore unfamiliar ideas, to admit self-contradictions, to slow down mechanical reactions. It is truth to refuse to fear anyone, to determine to think for yourself, to take a first small step toward inner newness."

REMEMBER

"Please review a principal task."

"Our task is to remember our cosmic homeland. It is like a boy kidnapped and then abandoned in a foreign land. While wandering around he remembers a wooded hill he used to climb at home, then recalls a favorite brook. The road to home comes back to mind, then details of the home itself. This remembrance guides him homeward. Likewise, we must remember our homeland nature. For example, at first we might recall our hidden talent for remaining calm when criticized. Or maybe we remember our natural ability to place the essential before the trivial.''

YOUR ROYAL ADVENTURES IN REVIEW

1. Apply these accurate guides to daily experiences.
2. A person needs only to get out of his own way.
3. Learn to value cosmic gold a bit more each day.
4. Know that a great turning point can be reached.
5. See how much help you can give yourself today.
6. Feel the enchantment of walking this true path.
7. A wish to understand is loaded with creative power.
8. Let your new nature create your new future.
9. Make a profound change in the way you think.
10. Start today to return to your cosmic homeland.